DEDICATION

To my family—Darlene, Derek, Dalisha, David, and Taylor—for always being the catalyst and foundation I have needed to continually "pursue the possible" with such vigor and passion, and for not ever knowing what it means to quit!

Also, to those in my life who have played an "elevator" role, those individuals who have worked closely with me to continually help me lift my life to higher levels.

To God, for never leaving or forsaking me, even when I appeared at times to be forsaking myself.

-Darryl Turner

THE NINE UNDENIABLE PRINCIPLES OF

UNCOMMON
—— $ENSE ——

A Dramatic Story of How a Team Can Work Together To

Stop Selling &
                  Start Believing

BY DARRYL TURNER
Foreword by Glen Berteau

Halo
Publishing International

Library of Congress Control Number: 2011915245
ISBN: 978-1-61244-041-5

Halo
Publishing International
www.halopublishing.com

Printed in the United States of America

FOREWORD

Forget Reality TV!

How about a reality book with *you* as the main character? Every thought, every action, and every event weaves through your present situation, exposing that insidious, crippling disease called "average." Will repeating the past ever satisfy your dream, or should you be creating your own future?

This book captures a journey into subpar production and dinosaur principles but with a "never quit" will to succeed.

Take a trip with the "real you" that no one sees—the insecure "inside you" that professes confidence on the outside. The one who has this thing called potential that no one sees, the one who keeps saying, "I don't get it. I am gifted to do this." What you need is a wake-up call in the form of psychological surgery and captivating analogies to propel your life and profits to new levels. What you need is *Uncommon Sense.*

Will Charlie (aka, *you*) become teachable? Will stubbornness prevail to the brink of poverty? Will shattered dreams become his (your) epithet?

Not only is the ability in you to make it but also the substance of success is there.

Glen Berteau, International Inspirational Speaker

"Dream Big, Act Out, Live Large!" ™
Darryl Turner

Let Darryl Turner Elevate Your Next Meeting

Hire Darryl To Speak
www.DarrylTurnerSeminars.com

Get Darryl Turner on Video On-Demand
www.DTonDemand.com

Books
Uncommon Sense (Halo Publishing, 2012)
Crazy Success (Morris Publishing, 2004)

For more information about
The Darryl Turner Corporation
and its programs and products,
visit us online at
www.DarrylTurnerCorp.com

CONTENTS

"It is always better to be considered horsepower than cargo."
Darryl Turner

PRINCIPLE 1

EXPERIENCE DOESN'T EQUAL SUCCESS

"Charlie, The Lousy Sales Guy"

This wasn't going to be just another Monday morning. Charlie had gotten up early today, as he was determined that this day, this week, would be better. He had firmly decided to work hard and not let defeat rule his life any longer.

Now it was 9:18 a.m., and Charlie had just left his second sales call of the day. As he stood outside the office building of his prospect, he had a single, powerful, resonating thought that kept running through his mind: *"That just wasn't fun! The previous sales call wasn't fun either! In fact,"* he continued to fume, *"why do I get all the lousy prospects? Why do all the other sales reps keep getting handed the better leads, the warmer prospects, while I keep getting these people?"*

Charlie proceeded to his car. Once inside, he mechanically began to fill out his call report. "Here we go again," he muttered under his breath. "One more time of trying to figure out what to write just in case someone actually looks at these things." With pen in hand, he began:

> Just left the office of George Ridener at Ridener Corp. The call went well. I introduced myself and we had good small talk to break the ice. I discussed some of our products and then proceeded to leave a price sheet. That was when he told me that they were happy with their current vendor and weren't looking to change. I will keep calling on him to see if he changes his mind.

He hesitated a second, then wrote a total lie, "Overall, I think this was a good call."

Charlie proceeded to start his car and back out of the parking lot. Looking over his shoulder while backing, he saw a sales rep from his competition walking toward the Ridener building. *"Good luck buddy,"* he thought cynically, *"You might as well just move along to your next prospect; this dude isn't buying anything."*

At 9:33, with the accumulated frustration from his first two calls, Charlie pulled into the parking lot of his next prospect. Unable to find a parking place anywhere close to the building, he expressed his compounded frustration out loud. Finally, he got out of the car, took a last quick look around for a better space, grabbed his bag, and began walking briskly toward the office.

Inside, with a bit of impatience, he greeted the receptionist. "Hi, I am Charlie with PazzCo. I would like to see Henry."

The receptionist, certainly a graduate of The National

Receptionist Institute, knew exactly what to say next. In fact, Charlie already knew what she was going to say because he had heard it nearly every day on nearly every sales call. He had come to hate her predictable words, "Do you have an appointment?"

Charlie answered the receptionist (now the gate keeper) with a simple "No."

In a nice but direct voice, she looked at Charlie and said, "You will, of course, need an appointment to meet with Henry."

"Yeah, that's what I suspected," Charlie said. "Any idea how to get one?"

She then reached to the top of the counter, picked up one of Henry's business cards, and handed it to Charlie. "All the information you need is on the card. I suggest you give Henry a call sometime next week and ask for an appointment to come see him."

With even more wind out of his sails now, Charlie reached out to take the card and managed a polite, "Thanks for your help today, I appreciate it very much." He then proceeded toward the door.

Walking across the parking lot, Charlie could not avoid thinking about all the pressures demanding that he make some sales. He thought of his boss, his boss's boss, his wife, the bank that held his mortgage and car loan, the utility companies . . . the list seemed unending. Then he remembered something else. *"Wait, that's why I got up with such vigor this morning. That's why I decided that today was going to be different."* He continued his personal pep talk with something he remembered hearing from his sales manager, *"I must just keep making calls—sales is just a numbers game."*

As Charlie drove toward his next call, however, he began to be genuinely puzzled. *"If sales is just a numbers game, then why am I not succeeding? I am making lots of calls on lots of people who have a need for what I have. Even a broken clock is right fourteen times a week! Why am I not succeeding?"* This thought began to really work Charlie over. The more the day went on, the more confused he became. *"Do people just not like me? Do they think I am not friendly? Am I not attractive enough? Do I smell? Is my haircut not working for me? Could it be that I need to buy a nicer car or a better suit? Am I making the wrong impression? Hmm, maybe it is me . . . nah, it's just a numbers game . . . at least, that's what my sales manager keeps saying, so I just have to keep hitting the streets."*

Pulling into the parking lot of his next call, Charlie's dilemma was still bouncing around in his head. "Snap out of it, Charlie!" he said loudly to himself in the rearview mirror. "You *must* be clear headed on this call—he's one of your best customers!"

Charlie got out of his car, walked toward the building and, once inside, noticed right away that something felt different. He walked through the door and greeted the receptionist. "Hi Sarah, how are you today?"

Sarah looked at Charlie and smiled. "Hey Charlie, what's up? Good to see you." It wasn't her words but something in her voice that didn't seem right.

Charlie went on back to visit the President of the company, a man to whom he has been selling for four years, ever since he had taken the position in sales. He actually had been handed the account from the previous rep who had decided to retire early.

"Hi John, how are you today?" he said with as much confidence as he could muster.

John looked at Charlie and replied, a little awkwardly, "Hey Charlie, I am, uh, fine, just fine, how are you?"

More than a little puzzled by his behavior, Charlie replied with a lie, "I am great! In fact, I wanted to come by to show you something new that we have."

Looking down at his desk muddles, John spoke. "Charlie, we really need to talk. I was going to call you tomorrow, but since you are here now, I guess there is no time like the present."

Charlie, whose puzzlement now had morphed into concern, sat down. "What is it, John?"

"Charlie, I hate to do this, but VallCo made us an offer we couldn't refuse. Now, I know you have called on us for years. I know our two companies have worked together, what seems to be, forever. But I have to tell you, they really have outdone you folks. Simply put, they came in here and just blew us away. I'm sorry, Charlie, I just couldn't pass this up. We are switching vendors. I really am sorry."

Like eddies in white-water rapids, numerous thoughts began to swirl around in Charlie's head. His concern went from disappointment straight to utter confusion. Hearing bits of his sales manager's training in his head, he knew he needed to ask some questions. "What did they offer you, John? I mean, I know we have competitors, but I really figured we had a great relationship."

"We do," John said. "This isn't a relationship thing at all. We really like you. You have always been friendly, courteous, and you come by a lot. It isn't that, Charlie."

"Then what is it?" Charlie asked.

"They just came in here and met with us and showed us some great stuff. Did you know that they have the lowest price on XB-48 frontal loaders?"

"They do?" Charlie asked, genuinely surprised. "I didn't know that." Still trying to remember his sales manager's advice for situations like this, he knew he needed to ask more questions. *"What are they!"* he thought frantically. He just couldn't remember the questions he should ask. So he continued to sell. "Yeah, but we have unbelievable service. And . . . we have free delivery . . . and . . . we will lower our prices if we need to. How much would I need to lower them to keep your business?" Charlie was now sick to his stomach because, although he couldn't remember the right responses, he knew in his gut that price was the wrong one.

"Charlie, I'm sorry. It is decided. Maybe when our contract comes up for renewal next year, you can have another shot at it. I am sorry, really sorry."

Numb from the news, Charlie got up from his chair, shook John's hand stiffly, and turned toward the door. Knowing he wouldn't see John for a while, he turned back toward him and impulsively said, "John, thanks for the business you have been giving us. Also, thanks for your honesty today. I know that what you had to tell me was difficult and I know it wasn't fun for you. I would like to apologize for even putting you in a position to have to do it. In fact, I missed it here. I didn't keep in mind that my best customer was someone else's best prospect. John, I am sorry." He then scurried out of the building as fast as he could.

Back in his car, Charlie's self-talk was escalating. *"What am I going to do now? I have serious bills due and this was my best account. I was really counting on them this year."* Starting the car, Charlie felt fully defeated. *"It is me!"* he thought. *"Numbers game, snumbers game! That's a bunch of bull. It is ME! I keep making sales calls, but I haven't been getting new accounts and now I am losing my good ones. IT IS ME—I AM DOING SOMETHING WRONG!"*

Driving back to his office, Charlie started to become angry. He was angry with himself, but he also was angry with his sales manager. *"It is his job to help me sell! It is his job to see where I need help! It is his job to hold me accountable,"* he thought.

The receptionist greeted him as he walked in. "Hey Charlie, Nick would like to see you."

"Nick?" he thought. *"Nick is the owner! What would he want?"*

After dropping some things off at his office, Charlie proceeded to Nick's office. It was on another floor, so he moved toward the elevator. Walking by the strip of offices along the wall, he noticed Kevin, another sales rep, carrying a box of goods from his cubicle. *"It looks like Kevin is getting fired,"* he thought.

"What's up, Kevin?"

With a giant smile, Kevin said, "Hey buddy, I just got an office!"

"Wow, that's awesome Kevin . . . what did you have

to do to get that?"

Expecting some kind of smart aleck response, Kevin instead looked at Charlie and lowered his voice, "I sell a lot of stuff, Charlie. I have been really using the system. Remember? The one we learned at the sales rally?"

For the second time that day, Charlie felt sick to his stomach. He honestly didn't remember the system. In fact, he hardly remembered the event and, even trying now, he had a hard time picturing the speaker. Mustering his most sincere voice, he said the opposite of what he meant, "Hey, that's great. I am really happy for ya, buddy." Patting him on the shoulder, he managed to add, "Keep it up, Kevin, great job."

Continuing toward the elevator, Charlie began to seriously hate his day. Thinking about his multiple bad prospects, the loss of his best customer, and now Kevin getting promoted, he shook his head angrily. *"Really? Kevin is getting promoted, and he has only been here less than a year? I have been here four!"*

The elevator ride to Nick's office seemed to take ten minutes, like the next floor was a mile away. Everything suddenly seemed to be in slow motion. Charlie was seriously getting mentally numb.

"Finally!" he thought as he walked off of the elevator on the executive level. Then a thought hit him, *"Wait, maybe I am getting a promotion, too! Yeah, that just might be it. If they can promote a guy like Kevin who's only been here a year, then certainly I'm on the list, too."*

Walking toward Nick's door, he noticed that his sales manager, Brian, was sitting in Nick's office. Charlie tapped on the open door. "You wanted to see me?" he asked with a hesitant excitement, thinking maybe, just maybe, things were about to turn around for him.

"Yes, come on in, Charlie," Nick said without emotion.

He proceeded through the door.

"Sit down, Charlie," Nick said.

He sat down next to Brian, who had not looked at him since he entered. He couldn't help but wonder why Brian hadn't even acknowledged his presence.

"Charlie, you have been here for four years," Nick began, "and in four years, I am guessing you would already know the opportunities that are in this company."

Charlie felt again some of his prior excitement. "Yes sir!" he said.

Nick continued, "That's why we wanted to talk with you." He paused, then said, "your numbers are not good."

Immediately, Charlie's emotions sank.

"In fact, we can't figure out what you do with your time. Why are your numbers so bad?"

Scrambling for words, Charlie began to answer with an involuntary stammer in his voice. "Well . . . um . . . I am trying. It is this crazy economy," he stated, knowing there had to be a better answer, but he really needed something external to blame because he didn't like the other option. "In fact, just today I lost my biggest account to the competition. Yeah, they said VallCo made them an offer they couldn't refuse. I am telling you, if we can't compete on price then this economy will really kill us!"

"Really? Is that your real answer?" Nick seemed to be getting a little upset.

Brian looked at Charlie for the first time in this meeting and spoke with a tone of impatience. "Charlie, if the economy has to be a certain way for us to make sales, then I really don't need you, now do I? The reason you are here is to play a role that elevates us above the natural levels of the economy. We want to win, but while your body is on the field, your mind is on the bench!"

With a nod from Nick, Brian continued. "Charlie, let's just cut through the whys and whats of your numbers. Get it together, or I will be forced to replace you. I don't want to, I really don't, but I can't carry you. You *must* get your numbers up. Now, I want you to go into your office and collect your things."

Now totally confused, Charlie sat stunned. A second ago, it sounded like he was getting another chance and now . . . like he was getting fired. "Okay, but . . . am I getting fired?"

"No, not yet. I want you to take your things from your office and move them into the empty cube across the room, the one Kevin moved out of. You and he will be changing places." Charlie looked dazed as Brian continued. "I just can't warrant giving you an office anymore. I need you back in a cubicle until you get your numbers back up. I'm sorry, but it has to be done."

Completely devastated, Charlie walked out of the office feeling like he had been kicked in the head. Not even remembering how he got down the elevator and back to his office, he shuffled slowly in auto mode until he arrived at the door. Inside, Kevin had started to unpack. "Kevin," he muttered, "I just . . . I just need to get my things."

Kevin looked at him with sad eyes. "I'm sorry, Charlie, I really didn't realize at first that this was your office. In fact, I didn't realize at all until I walked in and saw your things. I am truly sorry. Are you . . . um . . . fired?

Hanging his head low, he answered weakly, "No, not yet. Not yet."

While collecting his things, Charlie listened with annoyance to Kevin's attempt to cheer him up. "I'm not even really sure why they gave me this office; heck, I am hardly ever actually in the office."

Not missing an ounce of the irony, Charlie wondered the same thing. He stewed within himself as he began to fill a box. *"I am here all the time and Kevin is hardly ever here! This doesn't make any sense at all. Four years here—four times longer than this new guy—in a corporate office I worked hard to earn, and BLAM, just like that, I get his cube and he gets my office!"*

Charlie slowly collected the last of his belongings from his now former office. He couldn't help but wonder why Kevin was trying to be nice to him. In all fairness, Charlie had noticed on other occasions that the guy did seem to have an agreeable temperament. "That must be it," thought Charlie. *"Everyone knows that good salespeople are people persons. Maybe that's where I'm falling short."*

Then Kevin did it—he crossed the line. He really ticked Charlie off now. Looking up as Charlie moved toward the door with his box of belongings, he said, "Hey, Charlie?"

"Yes, what is it?" Charlie paused, looking at the ground deliberately, not turning his head.

"If you ever want help with your sales process, let me know. I am willing to help you."

Without saying a word, Charlie just walked out the door, fuming silently. *"Did he really just say that to me? The nerve of that dude! First he takes my office and now he wants to be my friend and sales coach?"*

Standing in his new cubicle, Charlie slowly took in the view. He remembered when he started four years ago and had a cube similar to this one. He also began to remember the excitement that he used to have back then. Nothing could stop him; he was going to set the world on fire. Well, in a word, he didn't.

He dropped his box onto the built-in desktop and sat quietly in the chair. Charlie then glanced over at the phone. *"What?"* he thought, as he looked just above the phone. Seeing a small piece of paper taped to the wall, he leaned closer to read it:

Remember the system. Sales is not a numbers game but a science. Salespeople are not born; they are built. They are a result of following proven systems that pay off. They are not people who visit or check in on customers or prospects. They don't start conversations with price. They look for problems to solve as every customer and prospect has them. If we aren't looking for them, someone else will find them and then fill them. Whatever you do, don't make sales calls without "The System."

> **"Sales is not a numbers game but a science. Salespeople are not born; they are built. They are a result of following proven systems that pay off."**

Sitting quietly, trying to remember more about "the system," or even the guy who presented it, Charlie was completely confused. *"Could this paragraph be why Kevin has my office?"* With his humbling undeniable, Charlie seriously wondered.

At 4:00 sharp, he headed toward his car, wishing the worst professional day he could remember would come to an end. He kept thinking about that small piece of paper on the wall of Kevin's former cubicle . . . or rather, his new cubicle.

Slumping down in his car, he didn't start the engine. Instead, he battled in his mind. It was an age-old battle between ego and humility, one that many ego-centered salespeople lose. It is the answer to this question:

Should I actually ask for help, or keep trying what I have been doing, even though it isn't delivering the results for me as I feel it should?

Charlie now remembered from an old training session the reason this question was so important. One's entire future is entombed within their ability to honestly answer that question and then act upon the right answer.

At 4:32, still in his car, Charlie picked up his cell phone and, shaking a little, dialed Kevin's cell number.

He answered on the first ring. "Hello, this is Kevin.

How can I surprise you today?"

"Hey Kevin, this is Charlie . . . listen, I have been thinking about what you said and, well, um . . . can we meet for coffee tomorrow morning at about 9:00 or 9:30? I want to ask you a few questions."

After what seemed like too long a pause, Kevin replied, "No, I can't do that. That is during my offense time and I am on specific appointments during that time. I would, however, be willing to meet you during some defense time. That would be between 12:15 and 12:45, and then again at 5:20 pm. Otherwise, if the morning would work better for you, we could meet between 6:00 and 6:30.

After a long pause of his own, Charlie answered, "Okay, yeah, let's do the 12:15 thing. I will see you at The Daily Grind."

"Okay, you have a good night."

"Yeah, you too, Kevin, good night."

*"The truth shall set you free, but first
it will likely make you really angry!"*
Darryl Turner

PRINCIPLE 2

ALIGNING THE SIGHTS

"You Don't Have an Income Problem"

Charlie's ride home that evening was strange, to say the least. He wasn't sure if he was supposed to be mad, concerned, sad, or what. He felt just sort of empty, maybe still a little numb from the day.

Walking into his house, his wife, Kim, greeted him with her normal, cheerful, "Hey, how was your day?"

"It wasn't good," he said flatly. "In fact, it might just be the worst day I have ever had, at least at work, anyway."

Instantly worried, her face began to lose color. "Were you . . . fired?" Kim asked as she fell toward the chair a short distance behind her. "What are we going to do? We have bills!"

"No, relax, hon. I didn't get fired . . . yet."

"What do you mean YET?"

"Yeah, that is what I mean when I say I really didn't have a good day. All I know is I haven't been fired . . . *yet.*"

It took a few minutes for things to calm back down between them, and then Charlie proceeded to tell his wife the story of his all-time worst day. He shared every detail, moment by moment, event by event. Something strange and unexpected happened, however, as he was relaying the events—he actually began to understand what had happened. He began to realize that he had lost his fire. He no longer took it all as seriously as he used to. He realized that his focus had been waning and he just wasn't in the game like he used to be.

"Did I just say *game*?" Charlie said out loud.

"Yes, honey, why is that important?" Kim asked, still quite concerned.

Charlie relayed bits and pieces he was remembering from conversations during the day. "Body *on the field* but mind *on the bench* . . . *offense* time and *defense* time . . . is it possible that my thinking is beginning to line up? I just said to you that I wasn't *in the game* like I used to be." Then it hit him, "If I am going to get back in the *game,* I must do what any good *player* does—learn, study, practice, huddle, and then, and only then, *play!*"

By the time they finished talking and had dinner, it was late. He kissed his wife good night and headed for bed. As he walked toward the bedroom, Kim said rather loudly, "Yes, but what are we going to do about your income problem?"

Doing everything he could to ignore the reality of the question, Charlie responded with a tired sounding, "I don't know, honey, I, I just don't know."

The alarm rudely interrupted Charlie's exhausted sleep at exactly 6:15 am. "Oh man, wow. This is way too early for me. If I could just sleep another hour," he grumbled half out loud. Then he remembered his obligation to Kevin and forced himself to sit up. Within 15 more seconds, he was out of bed and headed for the shower. Grabbing a towel, he turned on the water. *"Super hot,"* he thought, *"that's how I want it, hot enough to wake me up."*

After watching the news for a few minutes while eating a quick bite, he finished getting ready. By 7:30, he was heading out the door, calling goodbye to Kim from a distance. He really didn't want her to remind him again about their urgent income problem.

It was just a couple minutes after 8:00 when Charlie plowed through the office doors. *"Just a little late,"* he thought, *"so I just need to look like I am really trying to get here on time. Traffic. Yeah, traffic is the excuse of the day. If anyone asks, it was traffic on the 605."*

Arriving at his new workstation, he continued his self-coaching. *"Well, I better get this cubicle put together. I need to be prepared with a clean and organized environment if I am going to be productive out here in the middle of everyone."* He then spent the next three hours preparing his new space for his new mindset.

Charlie looked at his watch. *"It's only 11:00. What am I going to do for almost an hour and a half before meeting with Kevin? Wait, e-mail, I forgot to check my e-mail. Yeah, I need to clean out my inbox. I might even have something in there that is important."*

Finally, it was 12:00—time to begin the short walk to The Daily Grind.

Walking in the door, he looked around, thinking, *"What are all these people doing in here drinking coffee at noon? Don't they have jobs and responsibilities?"* Then he noticed Kevin, but he wasn't alone. In fact, the guy with him looked important. *"Is that suit a Versace? A Rolex watch? Who is this guy? Is Kevin interviewing for another job?"* Then he had a quick and selfish thought, *"Maybe I can get my office back."*

Kevin noticed Charlie and motioned that they were about to end their meeting. It was now 12:13. As the man got up to leave, Kevin called Charlie over and said, "I'm glad you're early. I would like you to meet Jerry Spangler. Jerry owns a sales consulting company with staff across the country. How many employees do you have now, Jerry?"

"We have, I think, as of 9:15 this morning, 216."

Charlie expressed dutiful admiration.

"Well, hey then, it was good talking to you, Jerry," Kevin said as he rose. "We will talk again in the next defense time slot, as I have an appointment now with my friend, Charlie."

"Nice to meet you, Mr. Spangler," Charlie said politely.

"Nice to meet you, too. Have a prosperous day." Jerry said.

The two sat down. "Okay, I have 30 minutes of defense time. I go back on offense at 12:45, so I can easily be back in the game and scoring by 1:00."

Charlie was starting to become a little irritated by all this offense/defense/game talk, but he tried to hide it. "Yeah, okay, anyway, I'm here."

After ordering coffee, Kevin spoke. "First, I want to tell you that I am truly sorry all this is happening to you. Why do you think things took this turn?"

There was a long pause. "I really don't know," Charlie said. "It all just piled up on me. And on top of everything else, now my wife is upset with me."

"Does she have a right to be?" Kevin asked.

Looking straight into his eyes, Charlie said, "I would love to say no, but the truth is I don't know. I am very confused right now. This all seems to have dropped on me like one bomb after another yesterday, and I just haven't been able to pick myself up yet."

After a couple of minutes of awkward silence, Kevin asked, "Tell me, do you really think this all hit yesterday, or could it have been building over the last several months, or even years?"

"Yeah, I guess it could, but I have been working. Really working. Sales call after sales call and still nothing. On top of it all, I lost my biggest account yesterday."

"No you haven't, Charlie. Your biggest account is at home hoping you get things together before the real bomb drops." Kevin paused, and then asked, "What would you say your biggest problem is?"

"Oh that's simple! My biggest problem is that I don't have enough income. And then that, of course, compounds my concerns and most likely takes even more from my ability to be productive, much less to be positive."

"Hmm, well I guess that sums it up."

"What do you mean, sums it up? Are you being sarcastic?"

"Not at all. We just discovered today why you haven't been able to fix your biggest problem."

"Hey man, stop the gibberish, already. Can you help me or not?"

"I can, but only if you will let me." Kevin paused, sipping his coffee calmly before saying, "I want to be the first to tell you that you don't have an income problem."

Looking at Kevin with sudden anger flushing his face, Charlie raised his voice, "Don't you dare patronize me!"

"I am not patronizing you. I am telling you the truth—and the truth will set you free, but before it does it will make you very, very angry! Just like right now. Now, if you would like, I will explain what I mean, but you really need to relax and just listen to what I have to say. Can you do that?"

Charlie grudgingly agreed but reminded himself he could leave at any time.

Kevin began what sounded like a polished presentation. "In life and in business there are three things we need to understand at all times. These are the three ingredients that make up every achievement we accomplish. In sales, these three things are the Economy, our Model, and the desired Results. Is this making sense so far?"

> **"There are three ingredients that make up every achievement we accomplish. In sales, these three things are the Economy, our Model, and the desired Results."**

"So far . . . go on." He motioned for the waiter to bring him a refill.

"Okay, here is what we have to realize, which by the way, the word realize means to have something become real to us—we must *realize*, for example, that we can't do a thing about the economy. Now, I know you know this, but worrying about it is a futile attempt to change it through the blame that's placed on it.

"The second thing we can't change is our results. Now, I know this sounds weird, but think about it. Results are . . . well . . . *results*. They are the end product from an action or set of actions. The bottom line is that we can't control them. We spend entirely too much time stressing, which by the way, is focusing on what we can't control instead of what we can.

"You see, the only thing we can control is our Model. Our Model is simply the process we follow to generate a result. Charlie, I must ask, because it appears to not be working, what is your process or model?"

Puzzled, Charlie answered, "I guess I don't really have one."

"Yeah, I would have guessed that but I had to ask." Pausing for a second to take a sip, Kevin continued, "Like I said before, you don't have an income problem.

Your income deficit is a result of your real problem. Your real problem is that you are simply following the wrong process. You are focusing on the item that can't be directly changed. It will only change as a result of working on what can actually change it, which is your model or process. I will tell you, without a doubt, that your problem is repairable if you can actually accept what it is. You simply need a new model."

Having sat quietly during the speech, Charlie finally spoke but in a low voice, almost a whisper. "The truth is, I feel like you just ran over me with a truck. I have my whole world caving in around me and now you are telling me I need to change everything I do? Really? I just don't think I have the energy to do that. I mean, maybe I should, but honestly, I can't even get my brain around it."

"Well, if you will let me, I will help you. But keep in mind, I am not going to break my own system to do it. I will only have certain times when I can help you. And—this may be the hard part—you will need to do everything I tell you, even if you don't want to or see why you should." At this point, Kevin looked squarely at Charlie. "If you don't, I will be done. Do you understand?"

"Yes, I do. I understand. I'm going to do it." After all, Charlie thought grimly, what do I have to lose?

"Okay then," Kevin said, checking his watch, "that's all the time I have. I gotta' get back on offense! How about tomorrow morning at 6:00, right here?" Before Charlie could even answer, he was gone. *"Well, I guess 6:00 a.m. it is,"* he assented silently. Then he groaned out loud when he realized just how early that was.

*"We blame the economy for low sales but don't seem
to give it any credit at all when things are hot!"*
Darryl Turner

PRINCIPLE 3

OVER RELIANCE EQUALS UNDER ACHIEVEMENT

"Letting Go of Help"

It was a rainy day and would have been a great day for Charlie to just roll over and pretend he didn't have anywhere to go. As it was, he was lying in bed contemplating his day and especially his early morning meeting with Kevin. In fact, he had been so anxious to get this thing going that he hadn't been able to sleep for more than a couple of hours. Normally, whenever he wasn't able to sleep right, he found that his best sleep happened after he hit snooze for the third time. As much as he wanted to indulge in just such a lazy morning, today he actually had been waiting for the alarm to go off.

As it turned out, the rain slowed his drive and he ended up running late. Dashing into The Daily Grind at 6:10, Charlie was surprised at how many people were there. *"I guess everyone wants warm coffee on a day like this,"* he thought. He found Kevin looking first at him and then down at his watch. He also noticed there wasn't any coffee on the table. "Charlie, you are late. Is this a good start?"

With guilt on his face and a desire to make excuses in his heart, Charlie simply answered with a grunt.

"Obviously, it's raining," Kevin stated, "So I guess we will have to do things fast, as we wouldn't want to get too wet. Where's your car?"

Puzzled, Charlie replied, "Kind of far out. What do we need my car for?"

Kevin gave no answer but just said, "Let's go."

They both ran to the car. Charlie unlocked it and quickly jumped inside.

"What are you doing?" Kevin shouted, still outside. "Get out here with me—open your trunk!"

As Charlie got out, he instantly began to get wetter. He started to get irritated, wondering what in the world Kevin was up to. "What is this all about? Why my trunk?"

"Open it," was all Kevin spoke, acting as if he were oblivious to the rain.

He opened the trunk, and Kevin looked inside and said only one thing, "Empty it!"

"What?" Charlie said, his irritation growing.

"Just empty it and then we will talk."

With the rain starting to come down heavier and the air almost freezing, Charlie proceeded to quickly empty his trunk.

"What are these?" Kevin asked.

"You know what these are. We all get them. They are promo items. Some are actually pretty cool giveaways. These are what my customers expect me to bring in on a sales call."

"Why is that?" asked Kevin.

Hesitating, and lowering his voice, Charlie said, "You know, I am not really sure, they just do."

"Could it be a learned behavior? Could you have taught them that this type of stuff is what you bring to them?"

As they continued to go through the trunk, they found more items that Charlie carried in on nearly every sales call.

"Get those bags there," Kevin said.

"You mean these plastic grocery bags?"

"Yes, grab them."

As Charlie pulled the bags from the trunk, Kevin looked him in the eye and said, "Toss it all. I want you to get rid of everything. Don't hold back a single piece, no matter how cool you think it is, or which customer or prospect you're sure would want it."

With great reluctance, and totally soaked by now from the rain, Charlie proceeded to toss items into the bags, filling one after another. He looked fondly at some of them that he really had no desire to part with, but in the end he did as Kevin directed.

"Now throw all the bags in the dumpster over there."

"Really?"

"Yes, 100% really!"

With greater reluctance, Charlie walked over to the dumpster and threw the bags in. Standing for a moment looking in, it felt for a minute like he was having a funeral for the bags and their contents.

After a short run back to the coffee house, where they stood under the awning out of the rain, Charlie looked at Kevin and said, "Okay, what's next?"

"That's it!" was all Kevin said.

The look on Charlie's face clearly displayed disappointment. He thought, *"I got up early, drove here in the rain, stood out in it and got soaked, then threw away hundreds of dollars of marketing items, and that's it?"*

"Why did I have to do this?" he finally asked.

"Listen," Kevin said in that speech voice of his. "I want to say this to you only once. Charlie, sales is not a numbers game and salespeople are not born; they're built. Whenever we rely on the types of things you threw away today, we have embraced what I call Growth Inhibitors. You have too many of them in your life. Let me ask you a question. If you never had items like this and knew you would never have them in the future, what would you have to do?"

Charlie was quiet and then answered, "I guess I would have to get better in sales is what I would have to do."

"Exactly, and that's why I call them Growth Inhibitors. They actually cause you to rely on items instead of skills. You get in the habit of walking in the door as the guy with free stuff, instead of walking in the door with a set of skills that actually can make you a living. In fact, until you disarm yourself and learn to let go of what you have relied on to help you, you have no growth potential. In other words, this is it my friend. You cannot grow beyond this point.

"But Charlie, you have made it clear to both of us that this level is not acceptable to you. So get rid of everything you have learned to rely on other than selling and business skill sets. While painful today, I promise that not too long from now you will certainly thank me."

> **"Get rid of everything you have learned to rely on other than selling and business skill sets."**

Charlie just stood there, hanging his head slightly to the left, but listening intently as Kevin continued. "In fact, Growth Inhibitors come in many shapes and sizes. In addition to things like these giveaways, there are a number of other things we learn to rely on that act as inhibitors."

"Really? Like what?"

"Well, how about the economy? Many learned to rely on it when it was hot. It was easy to make good money in sales when the economy was booming. In fact, for some the only things they needed were a pulse and a car. If they could get in front of a prospect, that prospect would buy. Now, notice how I didn't say they could *sell* to them. That is a whole other ball game. If people are buying and we are relying on certain Growth Inhibitors, then we aren't selling at all, are we?"

"I guess not," Charlie said, thinking hard. "I think I'm starting to understand. Like I'm not selling when another rep isn't doing well with an account so the company just re-assigns it to me, right?"

"Exactly. You didn't do anything to get that account; you were just handed it. Now you're getting it, Charlie, now you're getting it!"

Just then, Kevin noticed the time. "I only have a couple more minutes, so let's agree to meet tomorrow morning—same time, same place." Before he could even answer, Kevin was gone like a flash of light.

"Get rid of bad influences and negative thoughts.
Never medicate what you should amputate!"
Darryl Turner

PRINCIPLE 4
SELECTIVE LISTENING

"No News is Good News"

It was another early morning, something Charlie clearly was not used to. He rolled over in bed and wished he could just go back to sleep. Kim, on the other hand, was beginning to notice something different in him and wanted to encourage the changes taking place. "Get up, Charlie!" she urged.

"Uhh," he replied.

"Come on, get up! You need to get to your appointment. It is important!"

Charlie rolled over and looked at her with eyes half closed, then let out another loud grunt and pushed himself out of his side of the bed. "This is crazy," he grumbled. "Just a couple of days ago, I thought I was getting fired, and today I am jumping out of bed even before the sun comes up."

Today, however, he arrived at the coffee house a few minutes before Kevin. *"Hmm,"* he thought. *"Where is he?"* Then he looked at his watch and realized he was there at ten minutes before six o'clock. *"How did this happen? I am never . . . uh . . . early!"*

Right on time, Kevin walked through the door. He greeted Charlie and asked him to sit in the corner with his back to the large, flat screen TV mounted on the wall. "Say, I noticed you got here before me today. What's that all about?"

"I don't know," Charlie answered honestly. "It was weird, but somehow I just found myself here and I was early. Weird."

"So, tell me about your normal or typical morning," Kevin asked, "I mean, prior to this little game we've started."

"Well, I don't know . . . I get up and go to work."

"Come on, Charlie, tell me about your mornings. Seriously, I want to know."

"Okay, I get up around 6:45 and head for the shower. I take hot ones so I can really wake up. Then I proceed to turn on the news and get caught up on world affairs while finishing getting ready. I grab a quick bite, maybe a banana or something fast, and then I dash out because, honestly, by then I seem to be running a little late most days."

"So you usually make sales calls first thing, or do you end up in the office?"

"Sometimes I make calls but, to be honest, there are many days I just don't feel like it. I am . . . well, feeling a little unmotivated lately."

"Uh-huh, I understand. In fact, we all deal with that

at times. The key here is to minimize how often that happens."

"Now come on, Kevin, how in the world do you control your feelings, I mean, really!" Charlie was glad for the interruption by the waiter to take their order.

"Have you ever heard that your mind, your brain, is like a powerful computer?"

"Yes, I have and I agree. The human mind is truly amazing."

"Exactly. They are like mega-computers. If you think of the most powerful computer ever created, you still haven't reached the potential of the human mind."

"Agreed, but what are you getting at?"

"It's a simple answer, but first let me also ask you another question. Can you finish this statement: Garbage in, garbage ___!"

"Out!"

"Correct again, my friend. What happens when a computer gets corrupted files or, in some cases, viruses?"

"Well, it either crashes or just runs real slow. It can be maddening."

"Yes! So are you putting it together, yet? Your mind is a computer, and you have been loading it intentionally with viruses."

"Okay, now you've lost me. Can you translate that into English?" Once again, Charlie welcomed the waiter's interruption to bring their coffee.

"Okay, let me make it simple. There is actually a formula or flow to achievement. There are many things we carry both in our conscious and subconscious mind.

I am sure you would agree that your actions are the things that cause results, right?"

"Yes, of course, go on."

"Well, if it is your actions that create results, don't you think it would be wise to discover what it is in you that creates actions, or in some cases the lack of actions? You see, Charlie, the only real difference between any two human beings is the way they think. It is a fact—our life will never rise above our level of thinking. It is your thinking that controls your actions. Are you getting this?"

> **"The only real difference between any two human beings is the way they think."**

"I think so, but keep going."

"Okay, here is another fact. We only truly attempt those things that we believe we actually can accomplish. In other words, I don't care how much effort you plan to put into something—in reality you will only put all your effort into those things you truly believe are possible and probable for you. Can you grasp what I am saying to you here? I mean, is it really sinking in?"

"Yeah, I think it is making sense. Like when that guy broke the four-minute mile for the first time. Then, after that, a bunch of other people did the same thing, right?"

"Exactly—because nobody thought it was possible before. Then, Roger Bannister did it and, amazingly, a group of others immediately did it as well. The key to keep in mind here is that it wasn't thought possible.

Only when others saw what was physically possible did it become more probable for them."

Looking right into Charlie's eyes, Kevin became more serious. "Hey, tell me the truth, how have you felt the last few days of getting together with me?"

"I honestly am beginning to feel better, kind of like there is actually hope again."

"Then let me ask you another question, and I want you to think about the question before you answer. What is different the last couple of days from before, I mean as far as your routines go?"

"Well, you messed those all up, Kevin. I haven't been able to follow my normal routines at all, actually. I never get up this early, and I am certainly never out of the house this early. I would say, though . . . yeah . . . I like this." Charlie busied himself with his coffee cup.

"Have you noticed anything specific that is actually missing from your morning routines since we started getting together?"

"Nah, nothing specific, except these crazy hours you have me keeping."

"Nothing at all?"

"No, I don't think so. What are you getting at?"

"You told me that while you are typically getting ready for work, you watch the—"

Charlie finished his sentence. "—news . . . I watch the news."

"Yes, that is exactly what you told me. In fact, it is on right now, behind you, on that flat screen above your head. Don't look back at it—just know it is there. Have you ever noticed what types of things are on the news?"

"Well, let's see . . . the news?" Charlie was starting to get impatient.

"Is that all?"

"Okay, what are you getting at? This is getting weird."

Kevin took a leisurely drink of coffee, and then said, "The news doesn't discuss things that are going well or right in the world. In fact, they make their impressions on people every day by talking about all the things that are wrong, bad, or negative, and they have very few, if any, positive reports. Now, you told me the news is on while you are getting ready. Is it safe to assume that sometimes you aren't even really watching it?"

"Yes, I am usually rushing to get ready, so it is just in the background."

"Actually, that's worse! Remember the computer virus we talked about? Would you ever intentionally put a virus into your own computer?"

"Of course not!" he answered.

"Then how would it get there?"

"Well, it would come in through another source, an email or a web site, something like that."

Kevin became quiet and just stared at Charlie. "You mean it would work its way in under the radar? Is that what you're saying?"

Before Charlie could answer, Kevin leaned back in his chair and pushed his left foot closer to the table post. "My friend, that is exactly what is happening to you in the mornings. You are letting corrupted files into your mind each morning before you even start your day. These same corrupted files are getting into your mental hard drive under the radar."

It was Charlie's turn to become quiet. "Could that be why I am not motivated to make sales calls in the morning?"

"Not directly, but close. The reason you don't want to make sales calls is that you are emotionally out of balance. You are having a hard time getting your brain around having things go right for you or imagining getting more yeses on your calls. That part does come from the corrupted files—the viruses of negativity and despair." Kevin paused to let things sink in while the waiter refilled their cups.

"Think about it like this," he continued. "We already agreed that your results come from your actions and your actions come from your thoughts. What we haven't discussed, however, is where your thought patterns come from."

"Is this going to get even more weird?" Charlie asked, not sure how much more he could absorb.

"It might. What I am about to tell you, I am guessing you may never have heard before or possibly never even considered. Like everyone, your thoughts are generated by your influences. These influences are all rooted in your associations."

"What in the world is an association?"

"It is anything to which you literally, emotionally or, at least, mentally connect yourself. Negative associations can come in the form of watching the news, talking to the wrong people, and sometimes even from those closest to us. But this is what I really want to tell you—associations can also be positive. In other words, if you will begin to associate with other, different things, like spending time with positive people, not watching the news, searching for good economic news on the Internet, and other things like this, you can actually reverse this trend. Do you remember what I said earlier when I said your life will never rise above your level of thinking?"

"Yes, I remember."

"Well, since that is a stable principle, an irrevocable fact, then it is imperative that you install a powerful anti-virus application into your life, protecting you from the plethora of emotionally reducing viruses that will always be out there. Have you wondered why I insisted on meeting at 6:00 and dashed before giving you a chance to argue?"

"A little," Charlie admitted.

"Well, I did it because that is the time frame during which you have been watching the news. Tell me, are you still alive and well, not actually knowing what has been on your favorite news channel for the past couple of days?"

Charlie could not help but smile. "Yes, I am all good. I am all good."

Kevin stood up and reached to shake Charlie's hand. "Do you know what I am going to say to you next?"

"Back here at 6:00 tomorrow morning?" he said with a reciprocal smile.

"Right again, my friend. Think about all this and I will see you back here tomorrow morning at—"

Before he could finish, Charlie said, "—6:00, 6:00."

*"The second impression is simply
the first to be forgotten!"*
Darryl Turner

PRINCIPLE 5

THE FIRST IMPRESSION

"You Can't Compete Anymore"

It was 4:16 am. Much to his amazement, Charlie found himself lying wide-awake in bed in the complete darkness. Except for the occasional sound of a distant cricket or two, he couldn't hear a single noise.

"Charlie . . . Charlie? Are you awake?" Kim's sleepy voice expressed concern.

"Yeah, honey, I am. I have been lying here for a while now."

"What are you doing awake? It is so early!" Charlie felt badly about waking her.

"I just can't sleep. My conversation from yesterday with Kevin is really messing me up. In fact, I can't believe I am saying this, but this rookie is starting to get to me—I mean really get to me."

"You mean in a bad way?" He could tell she was waking up, however unwillingly.

Charlie hesitated. "No, Kim, not in a bad way, but

in a good way, a very good way. The things he has been telling me are starting to make a lot of sense. He really has me thinking. Could I actually have been so far off base? Is there really a better way to work and live my whole life? I mean he has me thinking hard."

It was now 4:55 and Charlie rolled out of bed.

"What? No grunt this morning?" Kim teased.

"Weird, but no," Charlie admitted. "Believe it or not, I am ready for the day."

Today, when Kevin got to The Daily Grind, he was greeted by a hot cup of coffee that Charlie already had bought for him.

"Hey, Kevin, what's up? I got you some coffee."

"Thanks, man, I appreciate that. I appreciate it a lot."

After some small talk, Charlie looked at Kevin and said, "Well, I have to admit you have really got me thinking. In fact, I can't even imagine what you might have up your sleeve for today."

Kevin laughed out loud. "Today. Hmm. Well, I'm afraid I have some bad news for you today."

Charlie's smile turned downward and he looked away. "Bad news?"

"Yeah, bad news. In fact, I waited intentionally until today, as I wasn't sure you would be ready for it until today."

Now, as puzzled as ever and very concerned, Charlie looked at him. "Well, give it to me, then. The faster we get this over with, the better off we both will be, I'm guessing."

Kevin reached across the table and put his hand on

Charlie's shoulder. "Here it is. Charlie, my friend, you are just not able to compete in the marketplace anymore. You actually don't have the ability. In fact, I am not sure if you will ever be able to."

With a very confused look, Charlie countered, "What do you mean? I can easily outdo my competition. I mean, with what you have given me so far alone, I feel like I can set records."

"That is exactly what I am talking about—that very statement. That is what I mean when I say compete."

Now more confused than ever, Charlie mumbled into his coffee, "Oh man, you are really acting weird this morning. You are making no sense at all. I really need you to explain. Are you trying to freak me out here?"

"Okay, there are certain things we take for granted. Some of those things actually create an environment where we simply are unable to compete. So I suggest you stop trying!"

At this point, Charlie started to get annoyed. "Kevin, you are just weird today. I can't tell if you are serious or if you are just playing with me. What I know is this isn't funny—not funny at all!"

In response, Kevin began simply to smile.

"Ah-hah! I knew you were joking. Dude, that just wasn't funny!"

Maintaining his smile, Kevin looked Charlie in the eye. "I am not kidding, though," he said. "In fact, this may be one of the most important things for us to talk about. Let me explain."

Kevin paused, then asked, "Can you tell me the first

time you ever kissed your wife?"

"For real?"

"Yes, for real. Can you?"

Taking a sip of coffee while trying to figure out what he was up to, Charlie answered, "Yes, I can."

"Okay, then let me ask you this—can you remember the second time?"

Puzzled, Charlie struggled with the question. He pondered for a moment before answering, "No, I can't."

"Why do you think that is? I mean have you ever thought about that?"

With this, Charlie started laughing. "You know, I can honestly say I have never wondered *why* I couldn't remember the *second* time I ever kissed my wife. Although I am sure I will always remember the strangest question anyone ever asked me!"

Kevin couldn't help but chuckle as well. "Yeah, you're right. I can see why it would sound weird to you. Okay, on that same note, let me ask you another question. Do you have a favorite restaurant?"

"I sure do, I love to go to Joe's. That place is awesome."

"Oh yeah, I have eaten there myself," Kevin agreed. "Tell me about the first time you ever went there."

Pondering, Charlie said, "Well, it was about six years ago. I was starving one night and could have eaten anywhere. A friend I was with said we really needed to go to Joe's. He told me I would love it and, frankly, he was 100% correct."

"Okay, then. Let me ask you even another question.

Can you tell me about the second time you went there?"

Charlie laughed again, and then leaned back in his chair, rubbing the bottom of his chin. "You know what? I really can't remember the *second* time I went there."

"Interesting," Kevin responded. "Why do you think that is?"

Still chuckling, Charlie responded, "That's another great question and, again, I am not really sure. I guess it was less eventful than the first time, perhaps."

The conversation continued a little longer, when Kevin asked Charlie, "Getting back to my question earlier, if you can't compete anymore, then what are you going to do?"

Confused again and borderline angry, Charlie blurted, "What in the heck are you talking about? I really have had just about enough of this gibberish. It's like you are trying to confuse me, which by the way is working!"

Kevin maintained an even composure. "When you make sales calls, how would you define the word compete? I mean, what does it mean to you to compete?"

"Well, it means to beat the competition." It was clear that Charlie's patience was being tested.

"Okay, well, how do you beat the competition?"

"That's simple, I find out what they are doing and then I beat it."

"You mean like on price, or what?"

Charlie felt more at home with these questions, so he relaxed a little. "Sometimes on price, but there are a whole bunch of other things, too. You know like free delivery, an extra stop for our truck to drop off special orders. It is simple—find out what the competition is doing and then do it better."

Sipping their coffee, the two men sat quietly for about a minute and half. The silence was starting to get a little awkward when Kevin interjected, "I still believe you can't compete anymore. It is clear that you are trying to outdo or surpass something that you did not first bring to the table. Let's relate it to your first kiss with Kim, or your first visit to your favorite restaurant. Nothing can remove that from your mind. In fact, the only way to have brand position or value position is to be the first to engage content.

"Charlie, trying to outdo the competition isn't competing at all, it is simply comparing. There is a huge difference. When you are trying to outdo the competition, you are entering into a world where you did not make the first impression and you have no value position in their mind. So, you are actually asking them to compare you with the other company. In the end, the most common way, if not the only way, to make the sale in situations at that point is to lower your price or to simply give up more than the other company is willing to.

> **"Trying to outdo the competition isn't competing at all, it is simply comparing."**

"The problem gets worse. Let's say you actually lower your price and make the sale and even get the account. Is this good?"

Paying close attention, Charlie responded, "Well, certainly not the way you are describing it, no, it isn't."

"The way I am describing it is objectively, just as the situation that takes place. Watch this—if you are able to make the sale and even get the account, on what have you taught them that your value proposition is based?"

"Price, I guess."

"Okay, then what do you think they will ask you for somewhere down the line?"

"Yeah, okay, I get it. I just taught them that I'm willing to adjust my price."

"Actually, it gets even worse. You will continually have to adjust your pricing to keep them happy. Why? Because your value is your price—your value is not based on the delivery of a single solution, just a lower price. Eventually, you will find the bottom where you just can't go any lower. Your customer, whom *you* trained, will then begin to shop you. Charlie, you will lose the account."

As these words hit home, Charlie's eyes began to brim with tears, which he quickly tried to shrug off. Looking Kevin right in the eye, he said, "This just happened to me this week! My best account told me that one of my competitors just made then an offer they couldn't refuse. I am still in shock! In fact, I am both hurt and angry. What do I do now?"

"When it comes to value and pricing, there are two things I want you always to remember. First, those who simply don't know what to do or how to sell eventually will find themselves lowering their price. Second, nobody knows the value of their own products or services as well as the one who is willing to provide them for less."

When the waiter started to approach, Kevin waved him off. He was on a roll.

"Okay, since you now know what comparing is— doing what others do and trying to outdo them—let's talk about what competing is."

"Okay, let's do that." Charlie was starting to get into the spirit of things again.

"Because we don't want to compare, to truly compete means we actually are going to do the opposite of what the other companies would do."

"What does that mean? I don't fully follow."

"When we do what others expect, they first compare us to other companies, and then they are quick to forget the whole event because we didn't surprise them and make an impression. We simply didn't stand out to them. Since value is perceived as that which exceeds our customer's or prospect's expectations, we must become extremely good at discovering those expectations.

"Most discover their client's expectations, so they know what to do, but I recommend you discover them to know where the starting point is or, in other words, what not to do. Ponder this—why do companies even exist?"

"That's easy, to make money."

"Correct and, of course, somewhere along the way, you taught yourself that by lowering prices you actually are helping them be more profitable. In fact, they readily tell you that, correct?"

"Funny, but yes. Many of my customers tell me how

much it helps them when I give them a better pricing level."

"How does it help *you*, Charlie?"

"It lowers my commission, that's how!"

"It also loses accounts for you, doesn't it? In fact, you will also notice that these very customers for whom you lower prices end up being the biggest emotional drain for you, too, don't they? So let me see, the ones who drain you the most, lower your commission, and then eventually leave you, are actually some of what you would have called, before today, your *best* customers. Am I right?"

With a humbled look, he replied, "Yes, you are. You're absolutely right."

"What I want you to do is to begin to ask more questions when you make sales calls. Don't answer questions so much, but ask them. Now, don't get me wrong, if it is a real question that requires an answer, then answer it, but make it a goal to operate around three core principles:

"(1) Discover their wants,

"(2) Develop a custom solution that solves the problems and gets them what they want,

"(3) Deliver this solution in a professional manner.

"You've got to stop going out and pitching products. Every product you have is designed to solve a particular problem for the customer. You'll soon get better at discovering solutions that way. When you offer products in the form of solutions that actually solve a problem, your customer immediately wants them. By the way, when they know what it solves for them, you will find that price hardly ever comes up."

"Make it a goal to operate around three core principles:
(1) Discover their wants,
(2) develop a custom solution that solves the problems and gets them what they want, and
(3) deliver this solution in a professional manner."

"Kevin, my head is spinning. I am completely overwhelmed."

"Good Charlie, good. I would rather have you overwhelmed than remaining where you have been for a long time, *under*whelmed. Hey, I gotta' run. We are not meeting here tomorrow morning. Instead, meet me at Beautiful Bouquet over on First Street at 5:20, after your offense time is over."

"Really, a florist?"

"Yep, I am going to teach you about flowers." Kevin laughed out loud as he walked backwards away from Charlie for a few feet before turning around and taking off.

*"Deliver an experience they didn't expect,
to create a surprise they couldn't predict,
to bring a result you couldn't imagine!"*
Darryl Turner

PRINCIPLE 6
THE 180

"You Will Need a New Product"

Charlie scurried through the office as he tried desperately to get everything done that would finish what he considered to be an oddly good day. He got up early, got ready for work, set his call schedule, and even his call objectives, all before leaving the house and without turning on the news.

Once at the office, he took the time to deliver a pleasant hello to Brian, his sales manager, causing a dazed look to fall over his face. Brian stared at Charlie, trying to figure out what was different about him.

"Charlie! Come back here," he called to his back.

"Yes?" Charlie said, turning around.

"What is going on here?"

"What do you mean?"

"I mean you! That's what I mean. You're acting different. And you look different. Is that a new suit?"

"No," he said with a smile. "It's not a new suit. I don't know what you might be seeing, but maybe it is the new me."

As he walked away, Brian's voice came from behind him, "I sure hope so, Charlie. I sure hope so!"

At the end of the day, as planned, Charlie arrived at the Beautiful Bouquet, where he saw Kevin talking with the owner.

"Hey, Charlie, come over here and meet Glen. He is a friend of mine. Yeah, that's right, I have a friend who's a florist," he added, as if to preclude Charlie's knowing look.

"Hello, Glen, it's nice to meet you. I'm Charlie."

"It's nice to meet you, too. So what do you two have planned?" Laughing, he said to Charlie, "He doesn't have you under one of his sales plans, does he?"

"Well, I think maybe he is trying to. I am almost tired of resisting. I'm about to give in." They all laughed together as Glen returned to work, and Kevin walked Charlie over to the greeting cards area.

"You know what these are?"

"Yeah, they're greeting cards."

"Of course they are, but what are they really?"

"You're doing it again, aren't you? Just tell me. It has been a super long day."

"Have you ever been in an argument with Kim?"

"That's a silly question. Of course I have—what guy hasn't had an argument with his wife?"

"What did it take to make up? In other words,

could you simply say 'Sorry!' and she immediately got better?"

"You don't know Kim, do you? No, it doesn't work that way at all in our home. In fact, sometimes it takes a day or two for her to cool off."

"When you say 'cool off,' what do you mean?"

"You know, to feel better again. To get back to normal."

This time it was Kevin's turn to look puzzled. "Did you say feel better *again*?"

"Yeah, why?"

"Well, feelings are what causes decisions. But feelings are not always based on facts, especially at first. Now, if they are not supported with facts, preferably sooner rather than later, then a new problem arises. Think about that new car you bought. Did you buy the one you needed or the one you wanted? In other words, did you spend over $11,000? Because, if so, you bought the one you wanted. Remember telling me about Joe's restaurant?"

"Of course, that is my favorite place."

"Why do you go there? Is it for the food or the experience? Let's face it, a can of chili and some crackers could fill you up, so why do you go to Joe's?"

"I guess I go there to enjoy the atmosphere, the people, and certainly to make sure I have nothing to clean after the meal."

"So, would you say that you go there out of need or want?"

"Oh, definitely out of want."

"Okay, you like to go to Joe's for *emotional* reasons." Using the universal "Shhh" sign, he said, "But nobody has to know that you have feelings if you don't want them to." They both laughed.

Kevin motioned Charlie to start walking towards a large glass case containing vases full of roses, where he asked, "Why do you think someone would want some of these roses?"

"I guess because they would make them feel special, loved . . . you know, cared about."

"Did you say *feel* again? Think about it, what other reason would anyone have to spend $75 for something they could grow in their own back yard for just a few dollars? The fact is, there is nothing logical about this whole floral business, nothing at all. So, why then do you think that Glen's business does well?"

"Hmm, I guess it is because men will be men—we'll say or do stupid things, and we'll always need to send flowers."

"Very funny, Charlie. Really, what is it?"

"Honestly, I don't know. Now that you mention it, the business makes no sense at all. None at all."

Kevin reached out and grabbed one of the $75 vases of roses and began to walk toward the cash register. "Are those for your wife, Kevin?" Charlie asked.

"No, sir, they are for yours!"

"Very funny, but I can't afford that kind of money on flowers. Get real here."

"Hey, buddy, yesterday you bought me coffee; today, I buy your wife flowers!"

In spite of Charlie's protests, Kevin paid for the flowers and turned toward Charlie. "Here, I want you to take these to your wife tonight. Give them to her and just simply say, 'I love you.' That's all. Are you listening to me? That's all!"

"I don't know," he said, still protesting, "they cost too much and I don't normally give her flowers."

"Exactly!" Kevin said.

"She will wonder what I did wrong! I just can't do it."

Kevin wasn't backing down. "Charlie, I am serious. Take these to Kim. Tell her you love her and don't say anything else."

"I am telling you, she will wonder what I did wrong."

"And why is that again?"

"It is because this is not normally what I would do—" All of a sudden, Charlie began to get it, and his words trailed off.

"Yes, she will first be surprised, which is exactly what you want from any customer—especially your best one. She will then worry for a second, which is an emotion, but in the end it will be the positive emotional touch that she will never forget. Remember, your goal is to make a permanent emotional impression on her. Do you get it? Simply put, only emotional experiences create deep, long-term memories. When it comes to your career in sales, how long do you want your customers or prospects to remember you?"

As they stood there with a vase of roses between them, Kevin asked another question. "Have you ever considered that when we sell a product we are actually working in the logical realm?"

"What do you mean? I am not fully tracking with you here."

"Well, when we are talking products, and features of those products, we are actually trying to make the prospect or customer see how logical this purchase would be. In other words, we are trying to make something fit into a hole we have yet to identify. Do you know what all this really means?"

"No, not fully, but I think I am starting to get it."

"It means that we can't win that way! So, if we are going to do the opposite of what the customer or prospect would expect, we are simply going to need another product. That's it, a different product."

"Come on, Kevin, we both sell the same products. You aren't talking about us finding different jobs are you?"

"No, I am talking about using all the same tools we currently have available, just taking a different approach."

With Charlie holding the vase of roses, both men stood in the aisle during an awkward silence. Charlie was not sure what was going on, and Kevin was waiting for Charlie's light bulb to come on.

"Have you ever been to the doctor?" Kevin finally asked.

"Yes, in fact I just went about two months ago. I had an ear infection."

"Let me guess, the doctor came in, asked you no

questions, and then proceeded to pull out his prescription pad and write you a prescription before sending you on your way?"

"No, I've never had a doctor visit like that," Charlie said, laughing.

"Okay, then tell me exactly how it went—don't leave anything out."

"Okay. First, after checking in, I waited. As I waited, I began to wonder if I was ever going to get in, and my ear hurt a lot. Then, after what seemed to be an eternity, the nurse called my name. She took me into a hallway and had me sit on this old green chair that looked like it came from the '50s. She then began to ask me some questions. Where is the pain? What else might I be feeling? Am I taking any medications? She asked a lot of questions. Then she made me get on a scale. From there, she took me into an exam room. I sat in the chair because I'm never comfortable sitting on the table with that perfectly smooth paper on it. Finally, the doctor came in. He asked me a few more questions, looked in both ears, and then proceeded to write on my chart."

"Did you feel like he was going to be able to help you?"

"Absolutely, he knew exactly what I was dealing with. When it was all done, he wrote my prescription and had his assistant call it in to my pharmacy."

Charlie was seriously starting to wonder what all this had to do with sales—and why in the world Kevin was making him take roses to his wife, only to create curiosity and possibly get him in trouble as, almost certainly, she would wonder what he had done wrong.

"Kevin," he asked, "seriously, what does this all have to do with my situation?"

"That's simple, Charlie. It has everything to do with it. Remember my first version of the doctor's visit, how it was wrong—the one about him writing a prescription before he assessed your condition? A doctor doing that is like you trying to push products because they meet a logical need, at least in your mind. When we discussed what really happened, you explained not only what the doctor did, but also how you were feeling during the visit. You see, this doctor was really helping you through an emotional experience. That is what works.

"For years, you have been trying to sell logically, and it is never going to work. Instead, you must identify real issues that your customers are having. Find the areas that present real pain within their situations. Then, solve those problems for them! When you do that, it won't be about price or what you can give them for free. It will be about the emotional solution you brought to the table. Have you ever heard the phrase, 'Get In Touch With Your Customer's Emotions'? This is exactly what I am talking about. When creating emotional experiences, we rarely remember those who serve us, but we always remember those who surprise us. Don't do what they expect—do what they don't expect."

> **"We rarely remember those who serve us, but we always remember those who surprise us."**

Walking out the door of the floral shop, it was now a couple of minutes before 6:00. Kevin reached over and handed Charlie something. "What is this?" he asked.

"It is dinner for two at Joe's. I made a reservation for you and Kim for 6:45 tonight. She is waiting for you at home but doesn't have any idea about what's going to happen. Charlie, this is your night. Go and see how well this all works . . . on your best customer."

Stunned, Charlie just stood there as Kevin said goodbye and turned to walk away. Then he turned back and said, "Oh yeah, one more thing."

"Yes?" Charlie wondered how there could be more.

"Have you ever had a sales rookie give you roses for your wife and a dinner for two at your favorite restaurant before?"

"No," he answered with a short pause, "I really can't say that I have."

Kevin then asked, "How do you feel right now?"

"Surprised—completely surprised."

As Kevin began to walk away, he asked, "Do you think you will ever forget tonight?"

"Only when I'm dead! And maybe not even then. Thanks, Kevin. This will help us a lot right now—more than words can describe."

"Honesty is always the best strategy!"
Darryl Turner

PRINCIPLE 7
POSITIVE SURPRISES ALWAYS EQUAL VALUE

"A Strange Day, Indeed!"

Charlie found himself walking around his house at a little after 4:00 in the morning. He just couldn't stop thinking about the dinner he had the night before with Kim, but especially how she had been so excited to receive the roses. In fact, his greatest amazement was that she seemed not at all suspicious or uncertain about why he had given them to her. Instead, she gleamed with excitement and kept saying, "Thank you, thank you," over and over again. It was like something inside her had been longing for this very thing. He had been wrong, dead wrong. He truly had misjudged her reaction.

Getting ready for work, he found himself sitting at the table eating a small bowl of fruit. He was casually thumbing through a book he had found on the end of the table. He worked his way through the whole book, glancing at about every other paragraph. Charlie was very relaxed. In fact, he didn't feel stressed about anything. *"Wow,"* he thought, as he realized how much he was enjoying the morning. *"What is happening to me? Why do I feel so relaxed?"*

Just then, Charlie's cell phone rang, pulling him out of his reverie. Looking at his watch, he noticed that it was only 6:07 am. Normally, he would let such an early call go to voicemail. This time, surprising himself, he answered with a cheerful voice, "Hello, this is Charlie, how can I surprise you?"

A voice on the other end said, "Charlie, this is Paul, you know, Paul from the warehouse."

"Oh hey, Paul, what's up?"

"Well, I am not sure what happened, but that shipment of XB-24 Collectors that was supposed to be delivered over to XES Corp . . . well, somehow they didn't make it. I am sorry, but I don't know what happened. Charlie, I just figured you would want to know."

"Yeah, yeah . . . I would. Well, I really don't want to, but I need to. Thanks for calling me and . . . when do you think they can get them delivered?"

"I will be delivering them myself this morning. They seem to have gotten separated when they came in on more than one pallet. Maybe that is where the confusion came in. I am going to round them up and then take them over there personally. I just wanted you to know."

"Wow, I certainly wouldn't have expected you to do that, Paul. It isn't even 6:30 yet, let alone 8:00. Thanks, buddy."

As Charlie hung the phone up, he found himself moving in slow motion. As the phone touched the base, he had a puzzled look on his face. As he turned away, he thought, *"That was weird. What a surprise!"* Suddenly, he caught himself and realized what he had just said!

"Man, that is what Paul just did to me . . . he surprised me. It is 6:07 in the morning and our warehouse person is there early, working on a problem affecting one of my customers. Wow! This is a really welcome surprise!"

Just then a thought hit him, and he quickly reached back for the phone. Speed dialing the warehouse, he waited anxiously as the phone rang for quite a while. Finally, after what seemed to be forty rings, a breathless voice answered the phone. "Hello, this is Paul. I´m here to help you."

"Hey, Paul. It's Charlie again."

"Hey, Charlie, what's up? Sorry it took me so long to answer the phone. I am the only one here. We don't actually open the warehouse until 8:00. Hey, I was just pulling the last of the XB-24s together. What can I help you with?"

"Well, I was just thinking about something. Tell me, what time will you be able to leave there with the delivery? I want to meet you at XES Corp. I am not sure what we might run into with this customer and just feel I should be there."

"I'm planning to leave here in just a few minutes. It's kind of a long drive and I want to be there by 8:00, as soon as they open. They were expecting these things yesterday. I really need to get them there before we create any additional problems for them."

"Yeah, you're right, Paul. I will meet you at XES at 8:00. Hey, do me a favor. If it looks like you might be a little early, or even a little late, will you call my cell?"

"No problem, Charlie. I'll see you there."

Charlie finished his cup of coffee, then reached over by the microwave and grabbed a few dollars he found sitting there. Stuffing them into his pocket, he slipped his coffee cup quietly into the sink, not wanting to wake Kim, and headed out the door.

"This is going to be a long drive," he thought as he hopped into his car. Suddenly, a memory flashed through his head . . . it was from his worst day at work ever, just a few days ago. He had been sitting in his car. He remembered shaking a little when he had decided to call Kevin to take him up on his offer.

Part of the flashback caused him to actually laugh out loud a little. He remembered what Kevin had said when he answered his phone—"How can I surprise you?"

"It's a lot like what Paul said," he thought. *"But that couldn't be . . . could it? Could Paul and Kevin be on the same path? Was Paul at that seminar last year?"* One thing for sure was that Paul certainly had surprised him this morning.

Thought after thought ran through his mind as he blasted down US-35 toward XES Corp. A little worried about what he might be walking into, he felt he needed to mentally prepare. "I need to be polite, apologetic, and honest. I will just admit what happened. Yeah, that's exactly what I am going to do." Just then, it was as if he could clearly imagine what Kevin might say, as if he were speaking in his ear. "Solve their problems—but before you can solve their problems, you must know what they are."

"Oh man, now I am hearing Kevin even when he isn't here. Scary, real scary!"

As Charlie pulled into XES, he saw his delivery truck backing into a stall near the end of the building. Jumping out of his car, Charlie jogged over to the truck. He jumped up on the side of the fuel tank that lay low on the driver's side of the cab. "Paul," he said, "thanks so much. You know, you really didn't have to do this."

"Yes I did, Charlie," Paul said. "In fact, we all have to do this type of thing. It is who we are." Just then Charlie felt like he knew exactly what was going on.

"Listen, I appreciate you taking care of this, I really do. But I have to ask, what is up with all this 'how can I help you' talk? Why is this 'what we all have to do'? I mean, have you been to some kind of seminar or something?"

Paul just looked at Charlie, raising one eyebrow out of curiosity. He said, "With all due respect, where have you been? Have you not noticed the economy? You know there are only two types of people. There are 'change makers' and there are 'change takers'. We just can't be okay with how others do it or how we used to do it. We need to get serious about our business. It's all about the customer. They are the most important part of this company. In fact, any company."

Charlie slowly stepped down, wondering just how far ahead of him Paul was. "Well . . . okay . . . go ahead then, open the back, and I'm going to run in and see if Mr. Fedling is here. He is going to want to know that his products are here."

"Okay," Paul said, "See you when you get back."

75

As Charlie headed into the front lobby of the building, he noticed a slightly odd, somewhat awkward look on the receptionist's face. "Hi," he greeted her politely, "I'm Charlie from PazzCo, here to see Mr. Fedling. Can you let him know I am here?"

"Sure, just take a seat right over there. Help yourself to some coffee, just around that corner to the right," she said, pointing.

"Thank you," Charlie said.

The receptionist got Mr. Fedling on the phone. "Mr. Fedling, there is a Charlie from PazzCo here to see you."

"He said he will be right with you."

"Thanks," he told her with a smile, "I appreciate it."

As Charlie thumbed through a magazine, sipping slowly on an overly hot cup of coffee, Mr. Fedling walked into the foyer. "Charlie? What can I do for you?"

"Well, Mr. Fedling, I wanted to come by personally to help resolve an issue. It appears that those XB-24s didn't get delivered yesterday as promised. I just wanted to apologize and also be here when they arrived. In fact, our truck is out at your receiving dock right now unloading them."

With an unhappy look on his face, Mr. Fedling looked directly at Charlie and said, "Yeah, I know they weren't delivered. In fact, it threw our whole team off by hours as they were scheduled to embed them yesterday. Do you know what it cost me to have my team on the line with no collectors?"

Nervous now, but trying hard to stay calm, Charlie said, "Actually, I really don't. I can only guess that it is a lot. I am very sorry this happened."

Mr. Fedling just looked at him. His anger seemed to be calming a little. "Why did you say you showed up with the truck this morning?"

"Well, honestly, I know how important it is for us to deliver our products. But even more than that, I wanted to make sure you were okay. I don't mean with us, as you are rightfully upset with us. I just mean in general. Mr. Fedling, I basically wanted to make sure you personally were all right, as I know this put stress on you. You are the reason I came."

Now looking more confused than angry, Mr. Fedling put his hand on Charlie's shoulder. "I will be all right. I do have to be honest with you, though. I have never actually had anyone say to me what you just did. It was a nice surprise. Has anyone ever told you that you are just a little different from the other salespeople?"

Looking for the right words, Charlie smiled and simply said, "I try; I really do."

Just then, Paul slipped in the side door in the hallway behind the offices. "Hey Paul, meet Mr. Fedling."

"My gosh, young man, what time did you have to get up to drive that truck all the way out here and be here when we opened?"

"Pretty early, Mr. Fedling. I just wanted to make sure we got these out to you first thing. I apologize. It was my staff that dropped the ball somewhere. I am not sure where yet, but I plan to find out so we can fix it and make sure it doesn't happen again."

Puzzled, Mr. Fedling said, "Well, thanks. I am not really sure what to say about all this, except I really appreciate it. You guys are just full of surprises, aren't you?"

As Paul turned to leave, Mr. Fedling said, "Thanks again, Paul, and it was nice to meet you."

"It was nice to meet you, too."

As Paul headed out the door to make his way back to the warehouse, Mr. Fedling looked at Charlie. "Hey, do you have just a minute?" he asked. "I want to ask you a couple of questions."

"Absolutely," Charlie said as they headed back in the direction that Mr. Fedling was pointing.

Arriving at his office, he motioned toward a chair. "Sit down, Charlie. Can I get you some more coffee?"

"No, but thank you for asking. You said you wanted to ask me something?"

"Yes, I did. What do you know about Stragistix as a company? And what about their main salesperson . . . what was her name again, Sherri, or something like that?"

Charlie found himself in a dilemma. On one hand, he sure could use a break and needed some good things to come his way, like recovering an account. On the other hand, he felt compelled to be honest. "Well, as you know, they are our competition, and I am sure they are nice people, but I am not really sure what types of things you want to know. Could you elaborate just a little for me?"

"Sure, Charlie. She came in here last week and brought her Regional Manager with her. The fact is that they made us an offer I don't feel like I can refuse."

Charlie started to sink in his chair. *"Is this really*

happening to me again?" he thought. Knowing that he really needed to be the one asking the questions, he said, "Okay, when you say 'an offer you feel you can't refuse,' what is it about the offer that stands out enough for you to feel that way?"

"I can save about 9% net if I switch to them. That can really add up. I probably shouldn't have told you what the percentage was, but I did. So, now it's out. I guess the question now is, can you do that as well?"

Taking a slow and non-obvious deep breath, Charlie thought fast. *"I can't have another situation like the other day. I have to handle this one differently. What am I going to say?"* He realized he was beginning to ask himself, *"What would Kevin say?"* Cautiously, he began to speak. "Can I ask you another question?"

"Certainly, what is it?"

"What are some of the things that could help your profits improve? I mean, other than the normal things you might talk with me about, what other things are there that you have to think about?"

Smiling, Mr Fedling leaned back in his chair. "Are you trying to get around my question, Charlie?"

Beginning to sweat, Charlie replied honestly, "Yes, I am. I certainly am."

With a loud and authentic laugh, Mr. Fedling reached over the desk and shook Charlie's hand. "Young man. Are you sure you are in sales?"

Not exactly sure about what was happening, Charlie responded, "Yes, I am in sales. Why do you ask that?"

"Son, you got up extremely early, came all this way

to make sure I was personally okay, and now you are being completely honest with me. Again . . . are you sure you are in sales?"

Charlie replied in a voice that reminded himself of Kevin, "One of the things I have learned is that there are only two types of salespeople. The first one does whatever they need to, says whatever they need to, and acts however they need to, in order to make a sale. The other type? They simply do the opposite.

> **"There are only two types of salespeople.**
> **The first one does whatever they need to,**
> **says whatever they need to,**
> **and acts however they need to,**
> **in order to make a sale.**
> **The other type?**
> **They simply do the opposite."**

"You see, I am not trying to make a sale. I am trying to create a customer. Unfortunately, the goal of simply making sales will cause people to go against the very principles that you or I would want to make sure were in place. They come in the door, not really concerned about how well your company is doing, or how you or your employees are doing. Instead, they only care about getting the deal, making the sale. I simply don't want to be like that. In fact, can I ask you to do me a favor? If you ever see me slipping, even a little, in that direction, would you tell me? I don't want to go anywhere near that path. It wouldn't be good for me, you, or any of my other customers. Would you do that for me, Mr.

Fedling?"

Sitting silently and staring at Charlie for what seemed like five minutes, Mr. Fedling finally spoke up. "I must say that you are a pleasant surprise. Honestly, I have never had anyone ever come in here and tell me what you just did. Charlie, I am seriously impressed. Actually, quite honestly, I am shocked. Completely shocked!"

Reaching over and grabbing a yellow copy of a pricing form from the top of a stack, Mr. Fedling leaned back in his chair and reached behind him. Next, Charlie heard the unmistakable sound of a paper shredder. "Charlie, I don't need that price sheet. In fact, it is in about a thousand pieces now," he said, laughing out loud.

"What I really need is someone who will always be honest with me, someone who will always be looking for ways to help me improve the efficiency of my company. I need someone who won't just say what they need to say, just to make a sale. In fact, I need someone who will risk making a sale just to make sure they tell me the truth and always do the right thing.

"It looks to me like I need someone like you, Charlie. Yeah, that's what it is—I need *you*. Don't get me wrong, I would love to save that 9%, but I have to tell you, the more I watched you today, the more I realized how different you are. You actually care. That price sheet I shredded? That was all they brought me. No other solutions or ideas, and they didn't even ask me what I really wanted. On the other hand, you risked it all today to be authentic. To me, that trumps a 9% discount any day. Thanks, Charlie. You actually reminded me of a few things I need to be paying more attention to. Honestly, I don't think I will ever forget this day. You caught me so far off guard, I don't think anybody would have the ability to forget this."

After wrapping up his meeting with Mr. Fedling, Charlie made his way back to his car. For the first time in a long time, he had a revelation. He realized that he really didn't need to worry about making a sale as long as he did the right things with all his customers, like he had just done. Naturally, he didn't forget that he still had to do all the things that make good salespeople good, and never forget to ask for the next level with each prospect and customer, but that wasn't the revelation. Today's revelation was simple. *"The rookie is really helping me,"* he thought. *"He is really helping me."*

He started his car and, looking over his shoulder to back out, he noticed Mr. Fedling walking quickly toward his car. Charlie rolled down his window. "Did I forget something?"

"You sure did, you forgot this." Mr. Fedling handed Charlie a file that was about two inches thick. "You know that new depot project on the north edge of town?"

"Yeah, I do, what about it?"

"Well, this is a copy of all the things we are going to be needing to complete it. I know this is a lot of stuff. In fact, this project involves more than we have bought from other suppliers all year. Charlie, can you guys handle it?

After a short pause, Charlie said, "No, I am sorry we can't."

The man's entire face changed. "What?" he said.

Charlie began to laugh out loud, "Just kidding, Mr. Fedling. I am just kidding!"

Mr. Fedling landed a friendly punch on Charlie's shoulder. "Get out of here, kid. Just get that stuff over here as soon as you can."

Both men laughing now, they nodded at each other and Charlie pulled away. *"What a strange day,"* he thought. *"What a strange day, indeed!"*

*"In order to face your future, you must first
turn your back to your past."*
Darryl Turner

PRINCIPLE 8
THE SECOND CHANCE

"The Turnaround"

A few weeks went by and Charlie continued to meet with Kevin on occasion. His days were starting to resemble, in one way or another, his pivotal day with XES Corp and Mr. Fedling. In fact, he seemed to be making a significant difference with all of his customers. It was as if he simply were a different guy; the old Charlie was completely gone.

Sitting quietly in their weekly sales meeting with his sales manager, Brian, Charlie curiously watched him, as he didn't seem to be saying much of anything noteworthy. In fact, Charlie intentionally wanted to stay in the background until Brian was ready for him to come back to the front lines. Thinking that he still wasn't happy with him, Charlie didn't want to further complicate an already sensitive situation by pushing himself into the limelight.

"Charlie?" Brian suddenly said in front of all the other salespeople.

"Yes, sir?" he replied.

"Charlie, what do you think about the new line of unidapters from UniCorp? Thoughts on getting some sales going on those things?"

Charlie felt this question to be strange because, other than a couple of brief conversations passing each other in the hallway, he and Brian hadn't spoken at any great length since the day he had lost his office.

"Well, I would love to tell you that they would be the best solution for our customers, but I can't."

Now somewhat confused and a bit irritated, Brian replied, "What the heck does that mean?"

In a respectful but serious voice, Charlie explained. "What I mean is that any salesperson who tells their customers that they have the best solution without first discovering their real problem would, at best, be just making something up. Not only is it the wrong thing to do, but it also doesn't work. Trust me, I spent the better part of at least three of the last four years trying that myself. What I found was it just doesn't work." Just then, Charlie looked across the room and saw Kevin sitting back in a corner. Without anyone noticing, he gave Charlie a quick nod.

> **"Any salesperson who tells their customers that they have the best solution without first discovering their real problem would, at best, be just making something up. Not only is it the wrong thing to do, but it also doesn't work."**

Without any expression, Brian replied, "Charlie, I would like to see you in my office after this meeting. Don't leave. It should only take a few minutes."

Charlie wondered if he had succeeded only in making Brian mad. *"Great, here we go again!"*

After the meeting, he headed over to Brian's office. As he approached, he saw that the door was only open about eight inches and he noticed Brian was on the phone. Before he could turn around to come back in a few minutes, he accidentally overheard him talking. "I don't know what that was all about. It was just flat out weird. Yes, I am going to get to the bottom of it right now. Something just isn't right here and I am going to find out what it is. Yeah, I will call you back after my meeting. Trust me, it won't take long!"

Charlie's thoughts raced. *"Oh, great! Really? Was he talking about me? I suppose I blew it this time— really blew it. Just when I finally seem to have a grip on my job and I'm actually doing what I need to do. This is just great!"*

Just then, Brian leaned over and looked through the opening in the door. "Charlie?"

"Yes, sir."

"Come in here, sit down."

As Charlie walked into the office, Brian buzzed his assistant, "Hold all my calls. I don't want to be interrupted."

Nervous, Charlie tried to appear relaxed, leaning back slightly with his legs crossed. Messing with the cuff of his left pant leg, he asked, "You wanted to see me, Brian?"

"Yes, I did. Look, I'm just going to cut to the chase. What is going on?"

"What do you mean by 'going on'?"

"Well, last month your numbers were horrible. You lost your office and almost lost your job. I have to tell you, I have been watching you. What is up?"

"Sorry, but I still don't really know how to answer your question. I'm not sure what you're looking for."

While staring straight at Charlie, Brian sat quietly for about ten seconds before finally speaking. "Okay, I am going right to the bottom line. I am completely surprised. Completely! It is like you have done a complete turnaround. Your numbers this month took you from 24th out of 27 salespeople last month, to 6th out of 27 today . . . actually, 26 now. So, either you are paying your customers to buy from you, or something very curious has happened. Either way, it is time you 'fessed up. I have been keeping an eye on you, and I just can't figure this out. So, tell me, what exactly is going on with you?"

"Brian, I'll gladly tell you what's going on, but before I can answer your questions, I have a couple for you."

"Okay, go ahead."

"First, how bad was I last month? Not just numbers but everything."

"Frankly, you were done. I was finished with you. Nick wanted to give you another chance. I didn't."

"I can't say that I blame you. In fact, I need to thank you for that second chance that you didn't want to give me, or I guess I should thank Nick. I want to ask you another question. Has the difference you have seen in me and my numbers solved the issue that you were having with me?"

"Yes, I would say that it has. But . . . you better keep this up, whatever you're doing. You are not completely off the hook yet."

"Fair enough," Charlie said, then continued. "So, were you thrown off by my answer to your question in the meeting? I mean, in hindsight, I think it might have sounded disrespectful. I didn't mean it that way at all. I was simply stating a sales principle."

"See?" Brian said. "That's what I mean. Where are you getting this stuff? Sales principle? Is that what you said?"

Charlie chuckled, "Yes, that is what I said. Sorry, I just can't see things any other way right now. I realized that over the last couple of years or so, I had lost my zeal. I had stopped selling and was just going through the motions. For that, I want to say that I am truly sorry."

Not quite sure how to respond, Brian said, "It's okay. Not the performance issues . . . but just the whole thing. It will all work out."

"Thanks, Brian. I really have been working hard. Really hard."

"Well, Charlie, it shows. Your numbers are good, your attitude is great . . . I'm still not sure I understand what happened, but I'm glad I didn't have to—"

"—fire me?" Charlie guessed.

"Yeah, fire you. Thanks for not making me do that."

"No problem, but I got fired anyway," Charlie said with a smile.

"What? Nobody can fire you but Nick or me, and neither of us did. What do you mean, you 'got fired anyway'?"

"Actually, there is one more person who can fire me other than you and Nick."

"Who? Come on. There is nobody."

"Well, there is, and he fired me." Being careful to not let this go on too long, Charlie looked at Brian. Leaning forward, he said, "Brian . . . I fired me!"

Brian leaned back in his chair with a confused expression on his face.

Charlie quickly explained. "In fact, I should have fired me a long time ago. Until I was ready to lose my ego and pride, ask for help, and sincerely work through the development of a new Charlie, I couldn't hire myself back. So . . . I fired the old Charlie and committed to a new process. I took full responsibly for my lack of results and committed to fix the problem. Since then, I have brought in seven new accounts and increased my overall sales revenue with my existing customers by 17%."

Pausing for a minute to let Brian digest what he was saying, he continued. "Here's the biggest thing I have learned through this whole thing. You may be my boss, but I can't be the best I can be for you, this company, any of my customers, or myself, until I become my own leader. I don't mean that in a rebellious way—in fact, just the opposite. I needed to get myself to a point where I was producing better results because of intentional changes inside of me. I had to want to be better and it couldn't be just about making sales. It simply had to be about always doing the right thing by the customer, you, and the company—and the right thing by me, as well.

> **"I had to want to be better and it couldn't be just about making sales. It simply had to be about always doing the right thing by the customer, you, and the company—and the right thing by me, as well."**

"The truth is, I needed be true to myself, and I hadn't been. I am now though—and now I am an asset instead of a liability. For that, I feel good. I also want to tell you that I am no longer behind you."

Hearing this, Brian leaned forward, leaning his face slightly to the right and looking sideways at Charlie. "What do you mean, no longer behind me? That certainly isn't going to work for me. Not at all!"

"Let me explain," Charlie said. "You see, if I am always behind you, then you have to keep looking back to see if I am still there. Instead, I need to understand your agenda and what you want to accomplish for this company. I need to be alongside you, not behind you. Not as a peer—you are my boss—but as a partner in initiative. I don't want to be cargo for you, Brian—I want to be horsepower."

They both just looked at each other for a few seconds, but Charlie could tell by Brian's beginning smile that he liked what he was hearing. He continued. "In addition to being beside you in initiative, you may find at times that I am actually in front of you, doing exactly what you would want me to do without you having to remind or even ask me. Does this sound like the kind of Charlie you would like me to be?"

With a big smile, Brian said, "You are just full of surprises, Charlie, just full of them. Okay, I've heard enough. Go on, get back to work now."

Charlie got up and started to walk toward the door when Brian stopped him. "Hey, before you go, can I ask you to do me a favor?"

"Sure, what is it?"

"You know that whole thing in the meeting about salespeople telling customers how our products can help them without knowing what they need or want, or however you said that—"

"Yes?"

"Well, could you take about twenty minutes at next week's meeting and share a little more on that and, actually, could I ask you to do a little training for the other salespeople?"

Charlie turned back, then reached out and shook Brian's hand. "I'd be glad to. That would likely elevate the whole staff, at least a little, and that would be good for them, the company, and even our customers. Yes, that's a great idea. I will help for sure. Thanks for the privilege—I would love to do it."

Charlie walked back toward the elevator to go back down to his cubicle. *"This is a great day,"* he thought. *"I am honored to be a part of some positive changes, which will be good for the company and everyone else involved. I really am experiencing a complete turnaround!"*

"Make a living, a life, or a difference.
The choice is yours!"
Darryl Turner

PRINCIPLE 9

WHEN THE PAST DIES, THE FUTURE LIVES

"Smashing the Itsy-Bitsy Spider"

It was a Tuesday evening, a little before 8:00, and Charlie was busy reviewing his notes for the sales meeting the next morning. While he wasn't sure exactly what Brian wanted to happen, he knew he wanted to pass on to the others some of the lessons he had learned from Kevin. Just then, to his surprise, his cell phone rang. "Hello, this is Charlie. How can I surprise you?"

The voice on the other end laughed at first, then said, "Hey, buddy, it's Kevin. What, are you trying to outdo me? How can you surprise *me*?"

At first taken back, Charlie then laughed as well. "No, Kevin," he said. "I am not trying to outdo you at all. In fact, I once heard a very wise man tell me that it was actually impossible to outdo anything that was first someone else's idea. At least in the customer's mind, anyway." They both laughed at this point, then enjoyed a few minutes of small talk.

Kevin asked, "Hey, man, are you wondering why I

called?"

"I am a little. What's up?"

"Well, I know you are about to share at the sales meeting tomorrow and—"

Charlie interrupted him, "—you don't want me to steal your thunder?"

Kevin laughed out loud. "Actually, it's not that at all. In fact, it's just the opposite. I want you to *take* the thunder. I want you to not mention me at all."

"Really, why? I mean, you have helped me so much. What is up with all this?"

"Listen, I learned a long time ago that it isn't about thunder—it's about *lightning*. In other words, I don't want to take credit for your success. I am just glad I was able to help you. Charlie, success or thunder is what we keep for ourselves, but significance or lightning is what we give to others. You see, you did it all—and now you have come full circle."

Charlie interrupted him. "Wait a minute here. You helped me all the way through. I couldn't have done it without you."

"I appreciate that thought, but the truth still remains that you did it all. I may have guided and re-guided you. I may have helped adjust your thinking, but you are the one responsible for all the actions that made all this happen for you. Really, just leave me out of it. This is your moment. Enjoy it. You've certainly earned it— every minute of it. Give them some lightning!"

As he hung up, Charlie began to think about what Kevin had just said. He wondered why in the world he would not want any credit for all he had done. He understood what Kevin had told him, but he struggled to grasp the concept of a guy not taking credit for something in which he had invested a lot of time and effort, and which had done someone else so much good.

As Kim walked into the room, she caught the dazed look on Charlie's face. "Are you okay?" she asked.

He replied, "I am . . . I am actually a little confused. Can I talk with you?"

"Of course you can, what's going on?"

"I just got off the phone with Kevin. He called me to ask me not to mention all that he has done for me. He actually told me not to tell any of them about all the help he has given me. You know that it was only because of his help that I was able to make the biggest turnaround of my life. Actually, the problem I have at the moment is honoring his request. I was looking forward to giving him some recognition—some much deserved recognition. I am not really sure what to do."

"Yes, you are. Come on, you are going to do what he asked, right?"

"Yes, I am, but it is going to be hard, as I organized my talk around his core principles—the things that helped me the most."

"Well, maybe just seeing you really start doing well is his reward. Maybe he just doesn't need the attention."

"Now you are starting to sound like him. This is too weird!"

"What I know is you'll figure it out. I know you will. Why don't you just sleep on it and see how you feel in morning?"

"Yeah, you're right. Let's hit it. I am tired and have gone over these notes enough. It isn't really what I write down, anyway, but what I have been living for the last month that matters. Let's go to bed."

"I love you, Charlie, and I believe in you."

Charlie looked at Kim. It had been a long time since he had heard those words. She often told him that she loved him, but the extra words were just what he needed. "Thank you, honey, and I love you, too, more than I can say."

Charlie's alarm clock went off at 4:50, but it didn't beat his excitement. He already had been lying there awake for at least thirty minutes. As he hopped out of bed, he heard Kim say, "This is your day, honey. Go make a difference!"

He was surprised, first that she was awake and second by what she said. "Hey, good morning. I am surprised you are awake," he said gently.

"I have been praying for you, Charlie. I know you will do great today but it doesn't hurt to ask God to step in and make sure."

Charlie smiled. "Thanks, Kim. I appreciate it. I appreciate it very much."

As he pulled into the office parking lot, Charlie noticed there didn't seem to be the usual number of cars. Confused, he glanced at his watch. *"It's only 7:10! How did that happen?"* he thought. *"I am early, real early."* He pulled into a closer space than normal and walked into the building, where he noticed Brian over by the coffee maker. As early as he was, he was not the first one there.

"Hey, Brian, how are you this morning?" he said cheerfully.

"Hey, Charlie, are you ready for our little meeting?"

"I am. All studied up." They both laughed.

"Hey, come see me in my office. I want to talk with you before we go into the meeting."

Trying to figure out what he might want to talk about, Charlie thought, *"Probably to go over my talk."*

"Sure thing. I will be right there. Let me grab some coffee first. Give me five minutes."

"Great, see you in five."

Charlie walked slowly toward Brian's office, looking at his notes with one hand and sipping coffee with the other. He approached the office, then leaned in as he knocked lightly on the open door.

"Hey, buddy, come on in."

"Buddy?" he thought. *"Hmm, this is weird. Not sure if he has ever called me that before."*

"What's up?"

"Well, I have some good news for you. And . . . well, some not so good news for Bill."

Charlie thought he knew who Bill was but wasn't sure. "Bill?"

"He's another salesperson here. He normally sits in the next to the last row in our meetings. He's the guy with mostly grey hair who almost always is busy emailing or whatever with his BlackBerry during meetings."

"Oh yeah, I think I know who you are talking about

now." Charlie couldn't help but wonder why Brian was telling him this confidential information. "Well, what do you have to discuss with me?"

"First things first. Take a look over there," Brian said as he pointed out of his office door toward the back corner of the sales floor. "See that office?"

"You mean the corner office?"

"Yeah, that's the one. Would you like it?"

Wondering if he was kidding or what, Charlie looked at him with a straight face and said, "No. I don't think so."

Brain took a full step back. "What? Seriously?"

Just then Charlie started laughing. "Of course I want it. Of course I do. Sorry, but I thought I would try that surprise thing one more time. Did it work?"

Brian was laughing now, too. "Absolutely. It sure did. You got me again, Charlie. Listen, I want you to move into your new office about an hour after today's meeting. I just need to have a little talk with Bill first."

Just then Charlie's heart sank into his belly button. He immediately felt the pain that this poor guy soon was going to feel. "What's up with him?" he asked. "That is, if you don't mind me asking."

"Actually, I can just tell you that he is not doing well. He is not even doing half of what I consider as his potential."

Charlie sat down on the couch, leaned back, and looked at the ceiling. "Brian, did you know that his potential is a variable? In other words, what he is actually capable of literally goes up and down depending on . . .

well, only one thing. Just one thing."

"I have to be honest, this sounds a little weird," Brian said. "Actually, it sounds a lot weird. But you know, you have earned the right lately. Go ahead and tell me. What is it that changes potential?"

Charlie looked Brian right in the eye and said, "Well, let me first tell you what doesn't change it—or rather, what doesn't change it unless something else happens first. I know we do a lot of training around here, but training on skill alone doesn't change potential. It's not a bad thing; in fact, it's a good thing, but it isn't enough. The biggest part is personal. What changes our potential first and foremost is actually *the level of our thinking*. Our business, life, and even our sales will never rise above our level of thinking."

Brian was caught completely off guard, because this actually made sense to him. He said with genuine interest, "Wow. That is deep, real deep. Where did that come from?"

Charlie smiled and then remembered what he was not supposed to say. Instead, he said, "It comes from a revelation that a very good friend gave to me."

Brian looked at him and just smiled. "This is all intriguing, Charlie. So intriguing, in fact, that I can't help believing it. It just sounds right. Tell me more."

Charlie continued. "The higher or more healthy we think, the more clearly we can see the possibilities in front of us. You and I won't do anything we believe we can't actually accomplish. We may go through the motions, but we are not going to give it our all. We want all of our salespeople to give their all, right?"

"Of course . . . continue," Brian said, nodding.

"Well, since we want people to give their all, then we must help them believe they can actually accomplish the goal they are pursuing. If we don't—"

Brian finished the sentence, "—we will have mediocre salespeople generating mediocre results."

"Exactly," Charlie said. "In fact, it gets worse. Those same people will never admit their problem. They will just keep going down the same road until they either find some new associations, or they get . . . fired. Sadly, too often they get fired." Charlie could not help but marvel that not long ago he struggled to understand Kevin's concepts and language, and now he was sharing them with his sales manager.

Brian chimed in, "Or they lose their office and move to a cubicle and somehow, miraculously, turn things around?"

"Absolutely, absolutely. That is exactly what I'm talking about!"

Brian looked at his watch. "Hey, we need to head over to the conference room. We only have about five minutes."

They stepped out of Brian's office and headed toward the conference room. They looked at each other with a look that said, without words, *"Let's keep the private parts of our conversation confidential."* Giving each other a nod, it was understood.

As the sales meeting began, Brian looked around the room, welcomed the sales team and then said, "Today, we are going to have Charlie share some of his thoughts on how to better move some product. If you remember last week, he spoke up and told us that we first need to determine the things that our customers want before selling them. Now, you might want to listen to this guy. I just spent a few minutes with him in my office, and some of the things he told me, well, they amazed me. So, listen to him and ask any questions you may have. Now, help me welcome him up here."

As he made his way to the front amid applause, Charlie surveyed the team. Then something crazy happened, something he never would have expected. As he looked at the sales team, he saw *people*. Not *sales*people but people. He saw real people with real fears—which fears, of course, most never would reveal openly. They were people with bills at home and probably not much in the bank. He noticed dads and moms and brothers and sisters. In other words, it struck him that the sales team was actually made up of human beings. *"Of course they are people,"* he silently reasoned.

Confused about why he was suddenly seeing his co-workers this way, Charlie paused for what seemed like ten minutes before speaking—even though it was really only a moment or so. It was as if he could feel some of the fears and pains that some of them were experiencing. Then he began, "What if we were the cheapest? What if we decided to lower all of our customers' pricing to a number that they picked? What if we were willing to do whatever they asked? Would you like that? I mean, as a salesperson, would you like that?"

No one on the team said anything, but instead they looked around at each other, wondering where Charlie was going with this.

"I'm serious. Let's not act like we wouldn't, at least at first, really like the thought of being the cheapest, the most flexible, and the most obliging to our customers' requests."

Kelly, a rep in the third row, popped in. "Yeah, that would be great. I am not afraid to say it. It would be great."

Charlie looked around at the rest of the room. "Who is with Kelly? Who thinks it would be great if our prices were lower?"

Brian was now looking at Charlie with a concerned look on his face.

"Look at Brian—he is scared to death at the thought!" Charlie laughed but with respect. "Don't worry, Brian. We aren't going to lower prices. Trust me, I have a reason for this." Brian now smiled, and put his hand palm up and forward with the universal "keep going" signal.

Charlie's eyes scanned the room. "Let me ask you all, what would lowering prices do for you? I mean except for cutting your commission and reducing your personal incomes. What would it do that is so important that you would actually want to do it?"

Kelly, who seemed to be the ad hoc group spokesperson, leaned back in her chair and said, "It would let me make the sale so much easier, that's what. Actually, I get a little sick of people telling me that our prices are too high."

Now someone else spoke up. "Yeah, it sure would. It would make my job so much easier."

Charlie turned to the white board. Not saying

anything, he drew a small circle on the left and a large circle on the right. In the smaller circle, he placed two letters. He first wrote the letter 'O' and then under it he placed the letter 'W.' In the large circle, he wrote the letter 'W' and under that he placed the letter 'O.' Then he turned to the group and stood silently while they looked back and forth between him and the board.

"So, what you are saying," he said, "is that you would like to lower sales *resistance*, right?" Thinking that lowering resistance meant lowering prices, half the room responded with an instant yes.

"So, if we lower prices, then resistance goes down?"

"Yes," the group responded, adding, "Yes, that would sure be nice."

He turned to the board, put his finger on the letter 'O' inside the little circle and said, "So, if we can reduce the **Obstacles**, then more people would **Want** to do business with us," pointing then to the 'W' in the bigger circle.

"In short, if we lowered our price, then more people would start using us, right?" The group was now both paying attention and in agreement.

"Let me ask you this," Charlie said, now that he had their interest. "Have you ever gone to a restaurant where the server didn't take your order, but just told you they would bring you what they thought you wanted?"

"Of course not," the group replied.

"So, let's see if I have this right, the server comes to your table, asks you what you want, and then proceeds to bring it to you, correct?"

Again, the assent was unanimous.

"Now, have you ever sat in a restaurant and tried to talk the server into lowering the prices on the menu just for you because another restaurant down the street offers food cheaper?"

At this, the group started laughing.

"So, let's apply this to ourselves. Is it fair to assume that if we can offer the solutions that people *Want*," pointing again to the 'W' in the large circle, "then their clear *Want* is large, just like this circle. What does that do to the way they see the *Obstacles*?" pointing now to the 'O' in the little circle. "What I'm talking about is to actually figure out what they *Want*—what actually solves their problems.

"It is like going to the doctor. When you are sick, you don't haggle about price with the receptionist before going in to see the doctor. That's all I am talking about. Listen, I am going to get to the bottom line. You are not going to like it, or maybe even me after I say it, but I have to tell you. The higher the sales resistance, usually on price, the less they see how what we have solves a problem for them. That's it! The bottom line! You see, price is all they think about if they can't clearly see how we are actually offering real solutions."

The room was dead quiet. Charlie paused for a minute, then continued. "I know you were expecting to discuss a specific product, but that really isn't our issue. Not knowing what our customers' problems are and what it would take to solve them—that is our real problem.

"The bottom line here is when the customer *Gets* more than they have to *Give*, a sale is always made. But the other way around? That's right, a sale is never made. Lowering prices doesn't increase what they *Get* at all—it just decreases what they have to *Give.* Don't ever be fooled into believing that this is actually helping the customer with a single problem except . . . well, getting you to leave."

Charlie looked over at Brian only to see him now taking notes. In fact, most of the team was now writing as fast as they could. Charlie continued. "Doesn't offering a real solution to a real problem also reduce resistance to the sale? This then is our problem—if we choose to be the cheapest and the most obliging, none of us will be needed." With this, Charlie paused while looking into the eyes of every person.

It was clear to him that they were paying serious attention to what he was saying. Looking at the team quietly trying to absorb the information, Charlie knew he had been in their shoes only a short time before.

He then said, "Why don't we all repeat this: 'My job is to bring a result for this company that exceeds what the economy alone will bring . . . in any market.' In fact, if I blame the economy or any other outside force because I simply can't get customers and prospects to open up to me and tell me their pains, then basically I am admitting that I can't do this job. Or, at least, I am currently choosing not to."

Just then, Charlie noticed a guy with grey hair holding his BlackBerry in his hand. He wasn't using it, however, just staring at him.

"This must be Bill," he thought. *"I hope he is going to be okay."*

The meeting continued. "Basically, we all have a decision to make. We must gain efficiency in our sales process. The only way to do that is to reduce resistance. Now, when we clearly understand the only two ways we can do this—lowering prices or offering authentic solutions—we will know which one we really need to do. We must get better at sales, of course, but first we must get better at thinking.

"I hope that this little bit of time has helped you do that. My first hope was that I would cause you to take a new look at lowering prices versus discovering wants and offering solutions. My hope was that you would believe. My next hope was that you would act and act immediately. We have great potential, but not if we are just looking for shortcuts. Those don't pay off for any of us—not at all. Now, help me welcome Brian back up here."

The team began clapping loudly. In fact, they all began to stand, one by one. As he thanked them sincerely, Charlie could not believe they were giving him a standing ovation. *"Could this really be happening?"* he thought. *"Just a few weeks ago, I was carrying my box of things out of my office into a cubicle. This is very hard to believe."*

Brian now stood in front of the team. "I am very happy we had Charlie share this morning. How about all of you?" The group clapped again. "In fact, he caused me to remember a little song that probably has been sung a hundred times in your house. I know it has in mine. The song is 'The Itsy-Bitsy Spider.'" The team started to laugh.

"Have you ever noticed that the song never ends?

The spider just keeps climbing up, getting washed out, and what does he do next?"

"He goes back up the water spout!" the team said in unison.

"Exactly. But notice that he keeps going back up the *same* water spout. Hey, everyone, have you ever felt like that spider? Here is what I would like everyone to do. Reach down and take off one of your shoes."

Each member of the team, a little curious, obediently took off one shoe. "Now, with that shoe in your hand, look at your folder in front of you. I want you to think of all the things you have done over and over again, and then over and over again some more, and never actually accomplished what you wanted to. Is everyone with me? On the count of three, I want you to take your shoe and hit your folder and smash that itsy-bitsy spider in you!"

The team smiled, as now they were getting it.

"Are you ready? One . . . Two . . . Three!"

Someone three floors up could have heard those smacks. The team started laughing and then the laughter turned into cheers. They couldn't remember the last time they felt so much hope. Brian now said, "Let's thank Charlie once again for being here and for sharing."

Before he could even finish the sentence, the entire team gave another great round of applause. As Charlie stood along the wall, feeling completely humbled, he caught Kevin's eye from across the room where he usually sat in the back. Kevin just looked at him and nodded the way two people do to silently say things like, *"Thank you,"* and *"You're welcome."* Kevin's look added, *"This was your day; I knew you could do it."*

The meeting had been over for about an hour when, all of a sudden, Charlie remembered! *"The corner office! I forgot all about it!"* As he looked around his cubicle, which had been home for several difficult weeks, he noticed the same little note up on the wall that Kevin had left behind. Slowly, he smiled and stood up. Walking toward his new corner office, he seemed to just stroll. On the way, he thought about where he had been not long ago at all. He thought about his new friend, Kevin, who had taken the time to transplant his life principles into him, and he thought about how he had insisted on no recognition. These were things he would be thinking about for a long time to come.

Stepping into his new office, Charlie walked in on an older gentleman sitting at the desk with his head in his hands. In front of him was a box filled with his office belongings.

"Sorry," Charlie said as he stepped back toward the door, "I can come back."

The man looked up and Charlie saw that it was Bill, the one with the BlackBerry habit.

"You don't have to go," Bill said. With a quiet voice, almost as if he were talking to himself, he said, "Brian told me it's your office now. I was just leaving."

With tears now brimming in his eyes, Charlie saw someone he recognized—he saw himself. He immediately remembered all his pain and all his fears. Walking slowly over to the chair on the visitor side of the desk, he asked, "You mind if I sit down?"

"No, go ahead." Bill sighed loudly.

Charlie sat quietly with him for a few minutes.

Occasionally, they looked at each other but didn't speak. It seemed to help Bill for Charlie just to be there.

After a few minutes, with a comforting, low voice, Charlie leaned forward and said, "What happened, Bill? What is going on?"

"I really don't know," Bill said. "I honestly don't know. I thought until today that the economy was taking its toll on my sales. That is, until I heard you at the meeting today."

"Are you getting fired?"

"No, not yet."

Charlie heard himself saying the same exact words just a short time back.

"Bill, are you willing to fix things? I mean are you willing to do whatever it takes to get things back on track?"

Bill answered, "I don't know if I can. I just don't know if it's in me anymore."

"You know, sometimes we have things backwards. We are taught that we are born, then we live, and then we die. Is that how you see things? I mean, it makes sense, right?"

"Of course it does; it's common sense," Bill said flatly.

"Exactly," Charlie said. "Exactly. You see, typically we are trying to generate uncommon results with *common* sense, but it's not enough. That is our problem—what we really need is *uncommon* sense to generate uncommon results! We have to see things in a different way."

> **"What we really need is *uncommon* sense to generate uncommon results!"**

A little confused but curious, Bill looked at Charlie and asked, "What do you mean?"

"In order for us to really advance toward our true potential, sometimes we must understand that, almost always, something has to die."

"Like that spider," Bill said.

"Exactly, not the actual spider, but what it represents in our lives. You see, step one is not birth but death. Something in us has to die before we can live. We have to let go of whatever is holding us back. It has to literally die. Then, when we actually kill that thing, whatever it is, we then go through a new learning process. It is that learning process that gives us hope. In other words, we start to change. Then, that change allows us to be re-born. In other words, we start a whole new life. Bill, I can help you. If you will let me, I can help you through this process."

Bill just stared at Charlie. Silent for a moment, he slowly started to speak. Holding back tears and with a quiver in his voice he said, "Would you? Would you help me? I really don't know what to do and . . . I think I am too old to start this whole thing over . . . I just can't lose this job. This is all I know. Please help me."

For Charlie, it was as if he were witnessing a live re-enactment of his own life not so long ago. Flashing through his mind, he remembered packing up his office, a rookie named Kevin, and all he had done for him. He remembered the early mornings at the coffee house, the trip to the florist, and learning the importance of lightning! In a way, it was as if Kevin had silently passed an invisible baton to him, and now it was his turn to pass on the priceless information that had saved his career. He had a clear and vivid picture in his mind of his first moment of change, and then he saw in his mind's eye a small piece of paper taped to the wall of Kevin's old cubicle. As if he were reading from it, he remembered every word because he now was living by its principles. Charlie leaned forward, looked Bill in the eye, and said,

"Bill, sales is not a numbers game but a science. *Salespeople are not born; they are built. They are a* *result of following proven systems that pay off. They* *are not people who visit or check in on customers or* *prospects. They don't start conversations with price..."*

THE END
—or—
THE BEGINNING

You decide!

ABOUT THE AUTHOR

Darryl Turner, international motivational speaker and founder/CEO of The Darryl Turner Corporation, has assisted over 100,000 individuals through his 100+ live events annually to develop more lucrative lifestyles, grow their businesses, and further enhance their relationships. Using his experiences over the past thirty years, along with the very strategies he has used personally to build a multi-million dollar personal and professional development and corporate growth strategies company, Darryl releases life-changing strategies and a look at what is necessary when it comes to creating change in one's life.

Through his strategies and processes, Darryl's clients have benefited from profit growths of over $80 million since the inception of The Darryl Turner Corporation in 1994.

Darryl and Darlene have been married since 1982 and are blessed with four beautiful children. They currently reside in California.

9 781612 440415